D1789657

Sewing
with Saint Anne

A Sewing Book for Catholic Girls
by Alice M. Cantrell

Little Way Press

Twain Harte, California

About the Author

Alice Cantrell has been sewing for over twenty-five years. While still in college, after studying advanced sewing and tailoring, she started a dressmaking business sewing for weddings and other occasions. After the birth of her first child, she converted her business to sewing custom-made children's clothing. She now sews only for her family. Alice currently lives in South Louisiana where she and her husband homeschool their five children.

Acknowledgments

I acknowledge three Persons in one God, I acknowledge the Pope as successor to Peter and the vicar of Christ on Earth, and I acknowledge Mary as the ever virgin Mother of God and Queen of Heaven and Earth.

I would like to thank my patient, loving, and supportive husband and children for putting up with the writing of this little book and making me feel as if it were something worth doing.

All the vintage clip art is, according to my sources and to the best of my knowledge, at least 75 years old and public domain.

The author in no way whatsoever assumes any responsibility for any accidents, injuries, or mishaps which may result from any tools mentioned or projects suggested in this book.

© 2002 Alice M. Cantrell

All rights reserved. With the exception of the patterns, which may be copied for family members only, no part of this book may be reproduced in any manner without prior written permission.

Cover design by *osprey*design, www.ospreydesign.com
Proofreading by Rose Decaen

ISBN: 0-9764691-2-X

Little Way Press
Twain Harte, California
www.littlewaypress.com

Distributed by Catholic Heritage Curricula
P.O. Box 125, Twain Harte, CA 95383
1-800-490-7713 www.chcweb.com

Table of Contents

This book is divided into three main sections. The first section contains the *lessons* needed to complete the *projects* in the second and third sections. Each lesson can be practiced as many times as needed.

Throughout the book you will find new terms which may not be familiar to you. Many of these words will be in *italics*. The definition of these words can be found in the Glossary beginning on page 83.

Some of the projects require patterns that can be found in the back of this book. The patterns can be copied onto regular copier paper and then cut out for use, or they can be traced onto tracing paper and cut out.

Anne, of whom was born the Mother of God.

Saint Anne, Patroness of Seamstresses,
pray for us!

A Note to Parents

The purpose of this little book is to glorify God, honor his beautiful servant Saint Anne, and, of course, teach young girls (and older ones too!) basic sewing skills. It is more than a "how-to book." Hopefully, it will help to enrich the Catholic faith of our daughters, while providing many opportunities to practice the virtues of patience and diligence. ☺ It is also my hope to awaken in our daughters a love of the feminine arts and of traditional homemaking skills.

A word about the tools and safety

A sewing machine is certainly not a necessity. After all, for hundreds of years women have managed quite well without them! However, in this day and time, if one wishes to cultivate a love and a talent for practical sewing, one might consider such a purchase. If the family already owns a machine, there is no reason your daughter cannot learn (by the age of seven or eight) to use this machine. If you do not own one, and funds are tight, consider purchasing a children's sewing machine which is usually about one quarter of the price of a new "adult" machine. Also think about checking into the adult "portable" machines that are small, easy to use, and fairly inexpensive.

A decent pair of dressmaker's shears is necessary in order to cut fabric. (This pair of scissors should be reserved for fabric only, as paper will quickly dull them.) *Please* use your discretion, judgment, and knowledge of the maturity of your child to decide whether you will allow her to use them with supervision or whether you will do the cutting out for her.

Most of the cutting your daughter will need to do will be the snipping of threads. For this task I have found the most useful pair of scissors for children to be "safety" or "nail" scissors. These are better constructed than typical children's scissors but still have a rounded point and are sized for smaller hands. "Safety" scissors can be found in the cosmetic or baby section of most drug and discount stores.

Ironing is another area in which this author relies on the parent to use her judgment. Hot irons with long cords and younger siblings are a dangerous combination. But you know your child. You, better than anyone else, can make the decision of whether to allow the child to do her own ironing.

In regard to pins and needles, occasional pricks to the fingers are an inevitable part of learning to use these tools. As your daughter's skills improve, so will her ability to handle these items.

Finally, this book begins at the beginning and assumes the reader has never sewn before. Almost all of the projects can be accomplished by an eight-year-old, but some, such as the very first lessons done on the embroidery hoop, can be practiced by girls as young as four or five.

Above all else, remember that mistakes *will* happen. Be patient with your daughter as our loving Father is patient with us. Just as we learn from our mistakes in life and become better parents and spouses because of them, so will your daughter learn from hers. *Allow* her to make mistakes and rejoice with her when she succeeds.

Note: This book is aimed specifically at girls in an effort to promote the fading, feminine arts, but boys can benefit from learning basic sewing skills, such as how to replace a button or mend a tear.

Before You Begin

Whether you have sewn before, or have
never picked up a needle, there are a few
things to remember before you start the first
lesson or begin your first project:

- First, collect all your supplies and keep them together in one area. This will save you much time and frustration.

- Second, these are *real* tools you will be using and you must respect them as such. They can and will hurt you if you are not careful with them. Never use them in ways for which they were not intended, and be *very* careful when using them in the presence of younger siblings.

- Finally, remember to *pray*! When you get frustrated and confused or you feel your patience wearing thin, ask Saint Anne to help you. She is Jesus' grandmother, Our Lady's mother, and the patron saint of seamstresses! She will ask Our Lord to guide your hands *and* your heart!

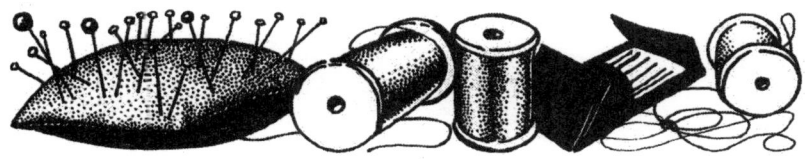

Your Sewing Basket

Your sewing basket can be made from just about anything!
A basket, a handy shoe box, or a pretty cookie tin. Use your
imagination. Look around your home for anything that will
safely contain the supplies listed below:

- A good pair of dressmaker's shears for cutting fabric. *(Do not use them to cut paper! This will quickly dull them!)*

- A pair of "safety" scissors for trimming threads. (See *Note to Parents*.)

- A seam ripper.

- A cloth tape measure.

- A set of hand-sewing needles—*sharps* or a *household assortment* (see "Different Needles for Different Needs," page 9).

- A pack of needle threaders—these are optional, but handy.

- A package of straight pins—the kind with the colored balls on the tops are easy to use.

- A few basic thread colors such as white, navy and natural. (A note about the cheap spools of thread: They break more often and can be *very* frustrating to work with. Better thread, such as *Coats* brand, is not a lot more in terms of cost but considerably more in terms of quality.)

- An assortment of buttons saved from old clothes that have been retired to the "rag box."

- A pin cushion is helpful to have on hand. You can purchase one, or wait a bit and you will soon be able to make your own. If you decide to buy one, the most common one on the market is the red "tomato" pincushion with the little red strawberry attached to its top. The strawberry is filled with emery powder to keep your needles clean and sharp. Just pass your needle through the powder once or twice before beginning a new project.

- The thimble is another item you might wish to have. But be careful, most of the thimbles on the market are not sized for smaller fingers.

- In the quilting section of craft supply stores, you can find chalk pencils for marking fabric. The white ones work especially well on the darker fabrics.

- An embroidery hoop is very helpful when learning new stitches. They are made out of wood and plastic, and they come in different shapes and sizes. For trying out new stitches and for large embroidery work, an 8- to 10-inch oval or round hoop works quite well. When working on something small, such as a monogram, a smaller hoop may be preferable.

Remember too, you should save any scraps from your projects in one convenient place together with your sewing basket. These scraps will be very useful when making smaller projects, gifts, and quilts. Also, when garments wear out and are no longer functional as clothing, inspect the item for any usable sections of fabric. If it is a pretty cotton print, for instance, think about using some for quilt pieces or doll's clothes. And don't forget to snip off and save those buttons!

 The Lessons

Below is a list of all the lessons in this section of the book. Although there are other "mini" lessons mixed in with the **Projects**, these are the main ones. Keep in mind that it is not necessary to complete all the lessons before starting your first project. If you encounter something in a project you do not understand, you can always go back and review an individual lesson.

 Threading the Needle

The very first thing you will learn is how to properly thread a needle.

1. First, cut a piece of thread about 24 inches in length.

2. Next, make sure the end of the thread you are going to start with is cut clean—this means no fraying. It is next to impossible to force a frayed piece of thread through the needle's eye. If you notice a rough end, trim it a little with good, sharp scissors to get a clean cut.

3. Now, hold the needle up to the light so that you can see the eye clearly. Then grasping the thread about an inch from its end, push it through the eye of the needle.

If you are using a needle threader, please refer to the illustrations below:

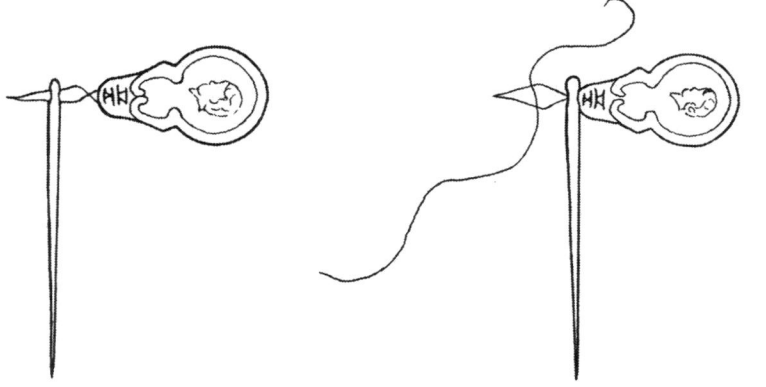

1. Insert the threader's wire loop into needle eye.

2. Push about 2 inches of the thread through the wire loop.

3. Now carefully pull the threader back out of the needle's eye.

Different Needles for Different Needs

The larger the needle size number is, the finer the needle will be. Select the needle size based on the weight of the fabric, finer needles for lighter fabrics and so on.

Sharps have small rounded eyes and are medium length. They are good for general purpose sewing and are sized 3 to 12.

Betweens are the same diameter and have the same size eyes as sharps, but they are shorter in length. These are sometimes called *quilting* needles. They are sized 1 to 12.

 # The Running Stitch

The running stitch is the most basic hand stitch. Even though it is certainly not a necessity, an embroidery hoop will make learning this stitch and others easier. (See "Your Sewing Basket" on page 5 for tips when buying a hoop.) Do not use a stretchy fabric (knit) for this lesson, but instead choose a woven scrap of cloth. Since this is only a practice exercise, the style of fabric is not important.

1. Now that your needle has been threaded, the next step is to tie a knot at the end of your length of thread. This knot will help anchor your thread to your fabric. The simplest way to begin is by catching *both* ends of the thread in a simple, overhand knot. (See fig. 4.) Try to make the knot end up about $1/4$ inch from the end of the thread, or simply trim the excess thread to $1/4$ inch after tightening the knot. This prevents the needle from becoming unthreaded accidentally and frees you to think about the stitches you are making, rather than worrying about keeping the thread in the needle. Later, you will master sewing with a single thread.

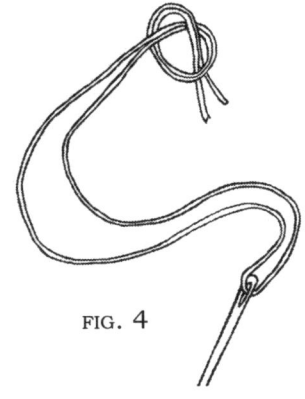

FIG. 4

2. If you are using an embroidery hoop, separate the two sections of the hoop. (If you are not using a hoop, you can skip to the next step.) Place the section *without* the tightening screw on a flat surface and lay a piece of fabric on top of it, making sure the fabric comes about 2 or 3 inches past the edge of the hoop on all sides. Next, place the slightly larger section (section with the tightening screw) on top of the smaller section to sandwich the fabric in between. The tightening screw may have to be adjusted to fit snugly. Make sure the fabric is smooth by pulling it if necessary.

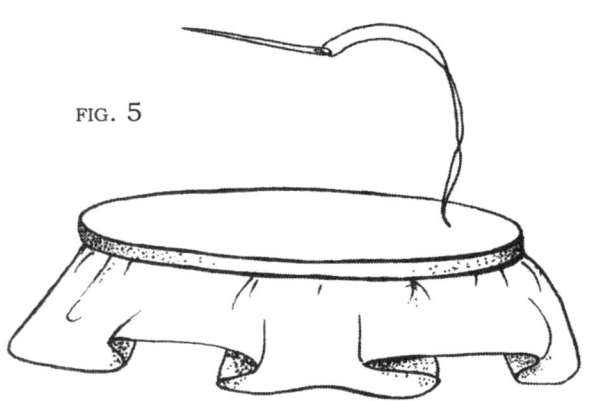

FIG. 5

3. Once you have prepared the hoop, or if you are not using one, you are ready to begin. Grasping the needle in one hand and the fabric in the other (and making sure there are no tangles in your thread), bring the needle up from the back of your fabric. Pull the thread slowly so that the knot at the end of your thread ends up on the underside of the fabric. (See fig. 5.)

4. At this point, it is helpful to use a ruler and a pencil to draw a straight line beginning at the point where the thread comes through the fabric, and going across the surface for about 6 or 7 inches. This guide will be a great help as you learn to make a straight line of stitching.

5. The next step is to secure the thread in the fabric by pushing the needle back into the fabric slightly behind where it just came out (see fig. 6), about an $1/8$ inch away or less, and then pushing it back up again slightly past the spot where the needle first came through (see fig. 7). This is called a *backstitch*, and it keeps the thread from being pulled out of the fabric. When making the backstitch, be careful to stay on the pencil guideline so that your stitches will be straight.

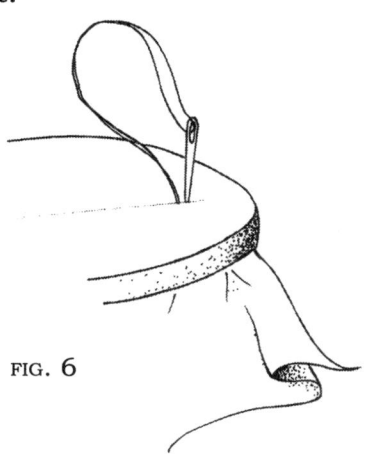

FIG. 6

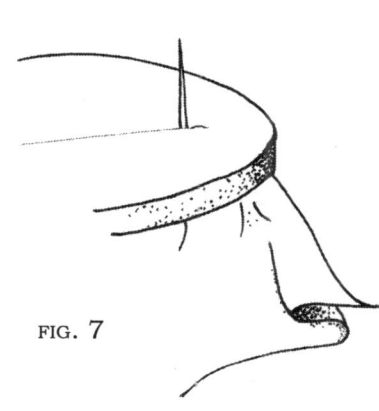

FIG. 7

6. Now you are ready to begin a basic running stitch. (See fig. 8.) Simply repeat the above steps, pushing the needle in and out of the fabric to make stitches no more than $1/4$ inch in length and taking care to stay on your guideline. (Don't worry if your stitches are longer; they will get shorter with practice. ☺) Be careful not to pull too hard on the thread. Pulling too hard will make your stitches gather and pucker. Keep the stitching smooth and flat as you go. Go as far along the pencil line as you can, but stop stitching before your thread runs out. It's always a good idea to leave about 3 or 4 inches of thread at the end of your line of stitching. *But do not cut the needle off the thread yet!*

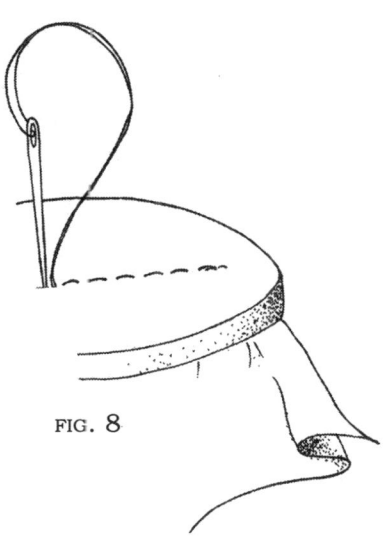

FIG. 8

7. Now the thread must be secured at this end of your line of stitching. There are several ways to do this, but one of the easiest is to simply make 3 tiny backstitches. When completing the last backstitch, make sure the needle ends up under the fabric on the wrong side. (This is so when the thread is cut the ends will not show on the right side of your fabric.) Now snip the thread $1/4$ inch from the fabric and place your needle in your pincushion.

 # Sewing a Seam

For this lesson, you will need two 4- to 6-inch squares of woven, cotton, or cotton-blend fabric—any of these types of fabric will work well. (Avoid stretchy fabrics, as these are difficult to work with.) Try to use up rags or scraps to avoid cutting up nicer, whole pieces of fabric.

1. First, cut two pieces of fabric into 4- to 6-inch squares. Iron them smooth if necessary.

2. Lay one square on top of the other with the right sides together and the raw edges even.

3. The area between the line of stitching and the edge of the fabric is called the *seam allowance*. (See fig. 9.) The recommended seam allowance for a pattern can be anywhere from $5/8$ inch to $1/4$ inch. Most mass-produced patterns use $5/8$-inch seam allowance, but many of the smaller pattern companies use a $1/2$-inch allowance. On this seam we will be using a $1/2$-inch seam allowance. It may be helpful to use a ruler and draw a pencil line $1/2$ inch from the fabric's edge across one end of your square. It is only necessary to do this on one square. This guide will help you to make a nice, straight seam.

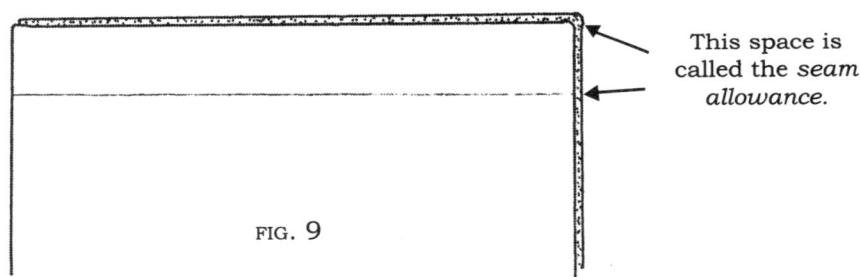

This space is called the *seam allowance.*

FIG. 9

4. Next, the fabric squares must be pinned to keep the two pieces together. Place the pins about $2 \frac{1}{2}$ to 3 inches apart along one side.

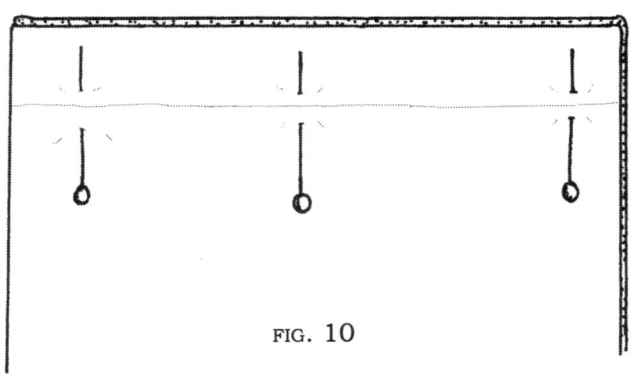

FIG. 10

5. Begin by inserting your needle on one end of your $1/2$-inch seam allowance line. Carefully pull the thread through the fabric until the end knot catches on the fabric. Be careful not to pull the knot all the way through the fabric. Now make a backstitch to help to anchor the thread.

6. Next, begin to make small ($1/4$ inch long or less) stitches while maintaining the $1/2$-inch seam allowance. With a little practice, you will be able to take several stitches on the needle before pulling it through. Carefully remove the pins as you encounter them. (See fig. 11.) *Make sure that as you remove each pin, you stick it back into the pincushion!*

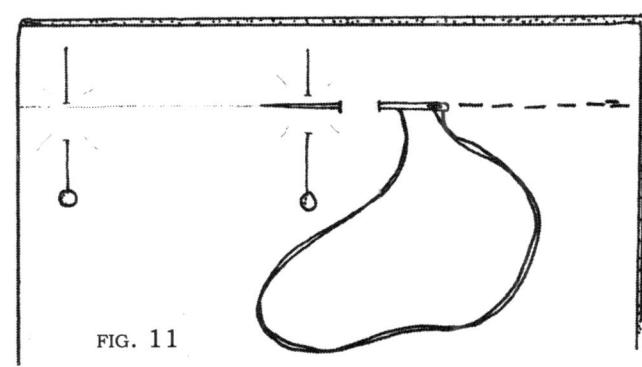

FIG. 11

7. When you reach the end of the fabric, make the 3 backstiches as before. If a seam is going to get quite a bit of stress, it is a good idea to also make a small knot after backstitching. (See fig. 12.) Snip the thread to $1/4$ inch after the knot and return the needle to the pincushion.

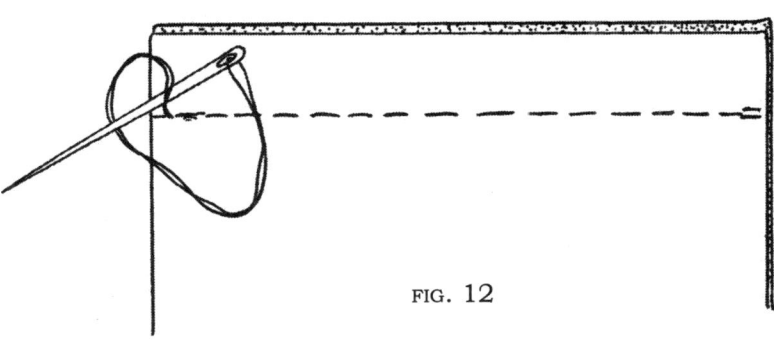

FIG. 12

8. The final step involves opening up the fabric. With the wrong side of the fabric face up, press the seam open. (See fig. 13.) This gives your seam a clean, polished look and is important when joining two seams together. *If you have never used a hot iron, please have an adult do this step while you watch!*

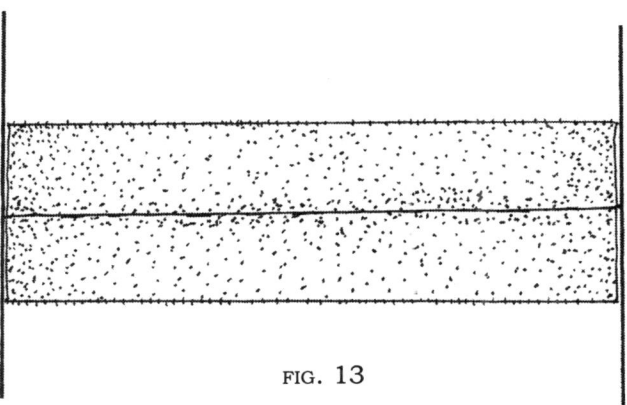

FIG. 13

Pins and Needles

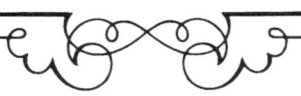

Needles have been in use for thousands of years. The earliest needles were made from fish bones and thorns. They were also carved from bone, shell, ivory, and wood. Eventually, needles were made from metal such as gold, silver, bronze, and much later, steel.

For many years bronze was the metal of choice for needle makers. Needle making was one of the ways fourteenth and fifteenth century European monasteries supported themselves.

A needle started out as a piece of wire. The needle maker then hammered one end flat and punched a hole in it for the eye. He filed down the opposite end until it was smooth and sharp. Needles today are still made in very much the same way, only today the metal of choice is steel and the needles themselves are made by machinery.

The production of pins was slightly different from that of needles. Most pins were hand forged, and the head of the pin was made separately from the shaft and then attached. It was a tedious and time-consuming process; as a result, pins were quite expensive.

By the sixteenth century, a lady quite often carried pins in small round *pincushion boxes* and needles in a little tubelike *needle case*. Both of these items were hung, along with other necessary items, on a *chatelaine* which was clipped to the belt of the lady of the house.

Saint Clare of Assisi,
Patroness of Needle Workers,
Pray for Us!

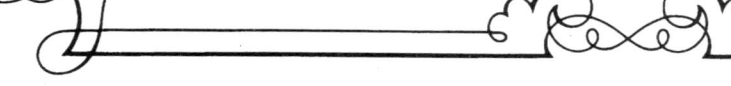

Using a single thread in your sewing will allow you to make finer stitches. As an added bonus, you will need to rethread the needle much less often.

1. First, thread the needle as you did in the first lesson but use a piece of thread 18 inches long.

2. Pull one end of the thread so that it is slightly longer than the other. Tie a knot in this end. Make sure you are only catching one thread in the knot.

3. The trick to sewing with a single thread is to hold both the thread *and* the needle when pulling a stitch tight. This way your needle does not come unthreaded.

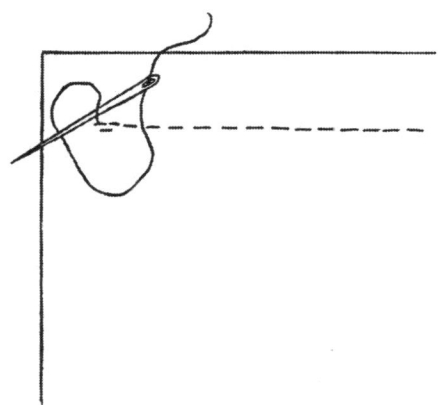

4. Beyond the differences mentioned above, sewing with a single thread is the same as sewing with a double thread. It will take a little practice at first to get accustomed to holding the thread so that it won't slip out of the needle, but soon it will come naturally.

Basting

Basting consists of large stitches that are made for the purpose of holding fabric together temporarily before the final stitches are sewn. The basting stitches will either be removed or covered up in some way.

1. All the steps for *basting* are the same as for regular sewing except there is no need for a secure knot at the end of your line of stitching. (See fig. 14.) A single backstitch will hold the basting long enough and still allow for easy removal later. (This is the same stitch used in gathering, except the single backstitch is not needed for gathering.)

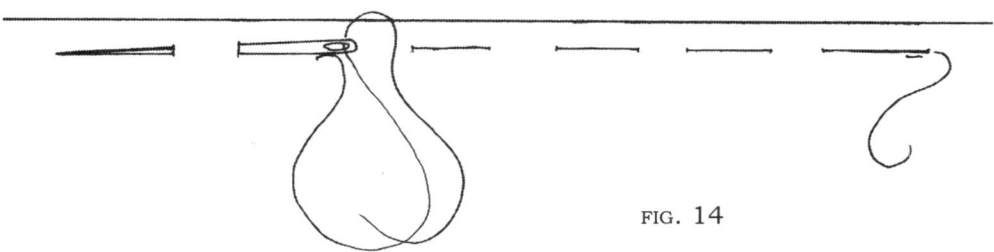

FIG. 14

2. Neatness in the stitches is less of a concern because they will not be seen. Make basting stitches about $1/2$ inch long unless instructed otherwise.

3. To rip out basting stitches, simply use your seam ripper to lift out the last stitch or two on both ends of the stitching and then pull out the thread.

Backstitching

The backstitch we are discussing here is slightly different from the backstitch you used to finish a line of stitching. This backstitching is used when an extra strong seam is required.

1. A line of backstitching can be sewn using a single or double thread. If the seam needs to be quite strong, definitely use a double thread.

2. After securing the end of the thread in the fabric, take one running stitch. (See fig. 15.)

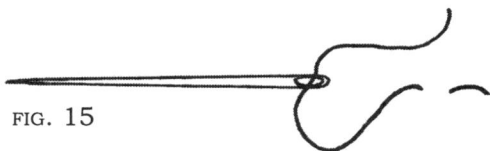

FIG. 15

3. Take a second stitch back to where the last stitch went in at the top. Bring the needle down and then up through the fabric about one stitch length ahead of where the needle last came up. (See figures 16-18.)

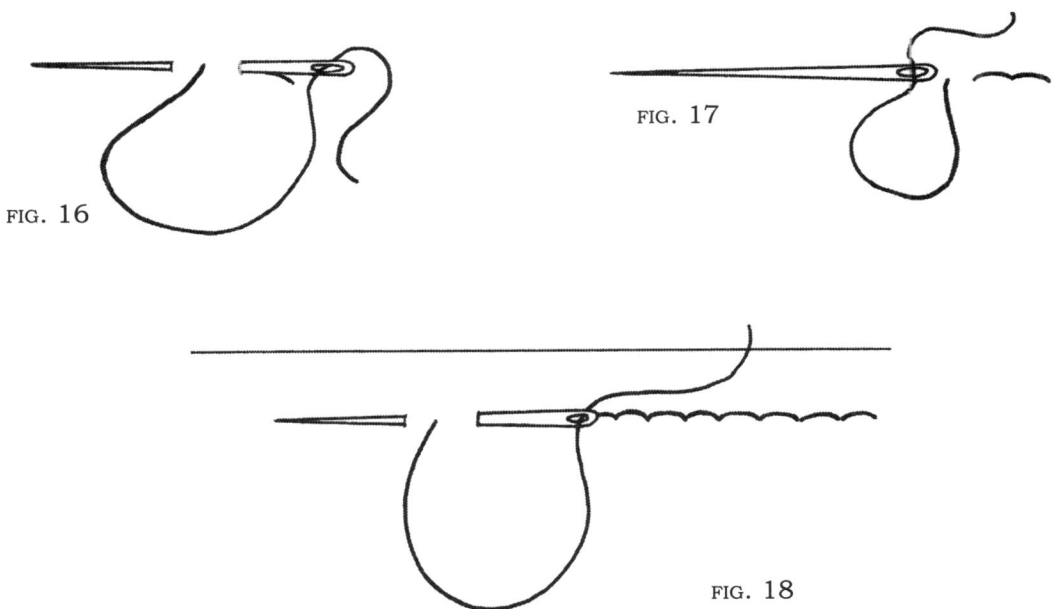

FIG. 16

FIG. 17

FIG. 18

4. Repeat steps 2 and 3 until you have come to the end of your seam. Finish it with 3 backstitches very close together or tie a knot.

The Chatelaine

The name "chatelaine" is a French word meaning "Lady of the Castle" (or of the "Chateau"). The chatelaine was a decorative medallion or plaque with three to nine chains falling from it on which hung various necessary personal items. The medallion was attached to the waist belt of the wearer with a clip or another chain.

The chatelaine became popular in the Middle Ages. The most common articles found on chatelaines of this time were keys, a needle case, a thimble bucket, and assorted bodkins. (The *bodkins* were needed for the many drawstrings and laces that were so popular in clothing of the sixteenth century.)

During the late eighteenth century and through the Victorian Age, chatelaines were *very* ornate and intricate and held mostly sewing tools and necessities. Items on a chatelaine of this time would include the previously mentioned needle case, thimble bucket, and bodkin; but added to that list would be a "sandwich"-type pin cushion, tape measure, pair of scissors in a sheath, and perhaps a tiny scent bottle. These chatelaines were made of steel, sterling, and occasionally gold. Some were even fashioned out of ribbons, fabric, and leather.

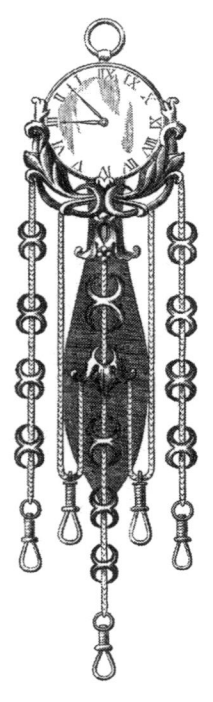

After the early 1900s, when women no longer wore their long full skirts, the waist chatelaine fell out of fashion. Today a version of the old chatelaine is still used by some seamstresses, but instead of hanging from the waistband, the tools of her trade are held in a pendant worn around her neck.

Overcast Seam Finish

A seam finish is the way in which the seam of the item you have stitched is sewn to prevent the material from unraveling. One common type of seam finish is an *overcast finish.*

1. To make an overcast finish, sometimes called a *whip stitch*, simply stitch the two seam allowances together with a slanting overcast stitch. (See fig. 19.)

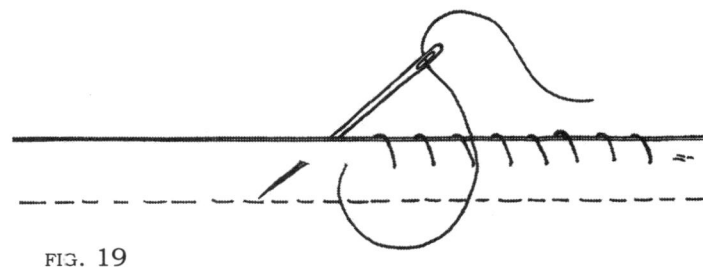

FIG. 19

2. Do not make the stitches too loose and be sure to keep them short. Make the stitches about $1/4$ inch apart.

3. If you are using a sewing machine with a zigzag stitch, you can zigzag the edge of the seam allowance for a machine version of the overcast finish. (See fig. 20.)

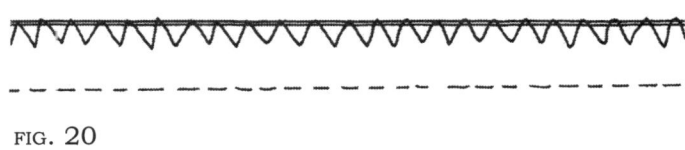

FIG. 20

Hemming

Hemming is the turning and stitching of the fabric that gives a clean finish to an edge. There will be two folds in making your hem and it is very important to press the fabric well after each fold to achieve a nice, smooth hem.

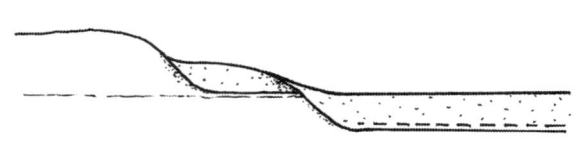

1. First, cut a 5 by 5-inch square of fabric that you can use for practice.

2. Carefully press $1/4$ inch of fabric toward the wrong side along one end of the square. (See fig. 21.)

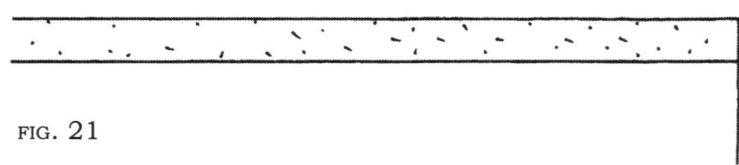

FIG. 21

3. Now turn the hem in 1 inch; then press and pin hem in place. (See fig. 22.) Although hems can be almost any size, we are using a $1^1/_4$-inch hem for the purpose of this lesson.

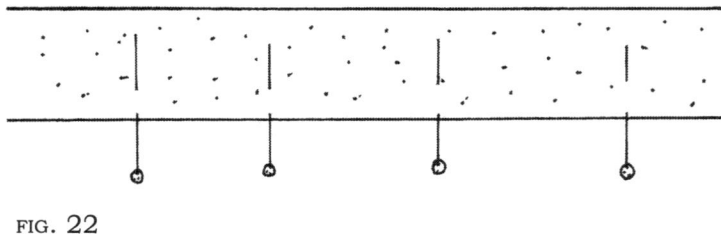

FIG. 22

4. You can use one of two main methods to sew the hem. The first method is called *blind stitching.* To make a blind stitched hem, first thread a needle with a single thread. Anchor (fasten) the thread securely by making 3 or 4 small stitches near the crease of the fabric which was folded over.

5. Begin by taking a very tiny stitch (about $1/_8$ inch)—picking up only 3 or 4 threads of the fabric the hem is being stitched to.

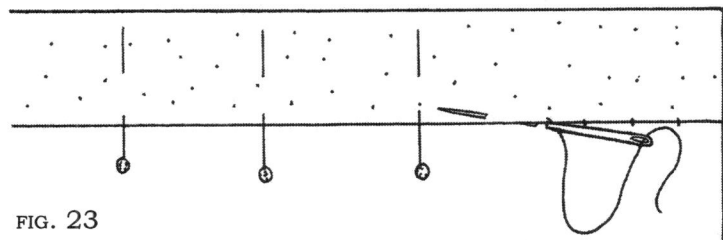

FIG. 23

6. After picking up the 3 or 4 threads, come back up through the hem about $^1/_2$ inch away. (See fig. 23.)

7. Repeat steps 5 and 6 until the whole length of the hem has been stitched. Make a knot at the end and remove the pins. Press.

8. If you now look at the right side of the fabric, you will notice that the hem is hardly noticeable, hence the name "blind" stitching. Blind stitch hemming looks nice on dresses and other items made from fine fabrics.

9. The second type of hem is *top stitching*. Top stitching is simply a running stitch that shows on the right side of the fabric. Prepare the fabric by pressing the hem in place and pinning.

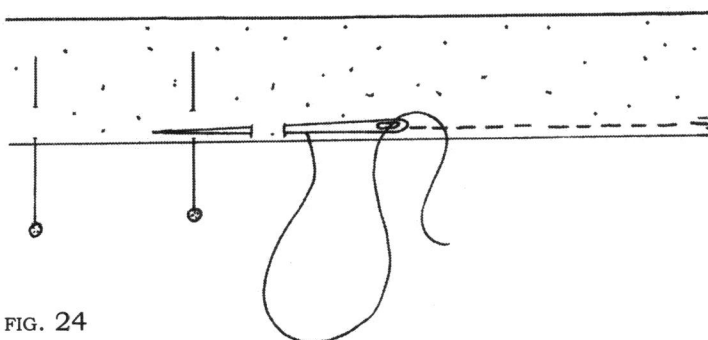

FIG. 24

10. With a single threaded needle, secure the thread at one end and begin a basic running stitch through all three layers. (See fig. 24.)

11. This type of hem is more visible, but it looks very nice on many things, such as casual dress hems, sleeve cuffs, and pockets.

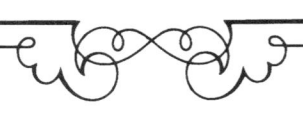

Saint Anne's Sewing Circle

Years ago sewing circles were a very popular way for ladies, both young and old, to visit with friends and neighbors while keeping their hands busy with valuable work. These meetings were especially popular in the late 1700s and 1800s.

Ladies would gather at a different home for each meeting and bring whatever sewing project they were currently working on, including embroidery work, quilting, mending, or plain sewing. The hostess of a particular meeting would provide refreshments such as tea, lemonade, cookies, cakes, and little sandwiches.

Most of the sewing groups were informal gatherings of friends, but sometimes they were more formal—minutes (notes) would be taken for each meeting. Such formal sewing circles usually were formed to provide sewing for a specific need, such as bedding for a charity hospital during a time of war.

After you become comfortable with your new sewing skills, consider continuing the tradition of the sewing circle by starting your own. It is a chance to share what you have learned with friends and to learn new stitches and techniques yourself. Hosting such a gathering also provides you with an opportunity to practice hospitality. You can dedicate your circle to Saint Anne, as she is the patron saint of seamstresses, or to the Blessed Mother or *any* other favorite saint!

Good Saint Anne,
Pray for Us!

⊰⊱ Ripping Out Stitches ⊰⊱

Mistakes will happen, but thankfully, sewing is a *very* forgiving art. ☺

1. Hopefully your sewing basket already contains one of these very handy tools, a seam ripper:

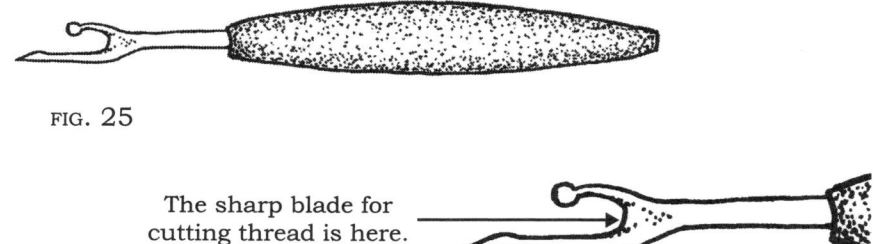

FIG. 25

The sharp blade for cutting thread is here. ⟶

2. It is quite easy to rip out a section of stitching that may not have turned out just right. Simply slide the point of the seam ripper under a stitch until the thread is against the blade area of the tool. With a firm push and slight lift, you should easily cut the thread.

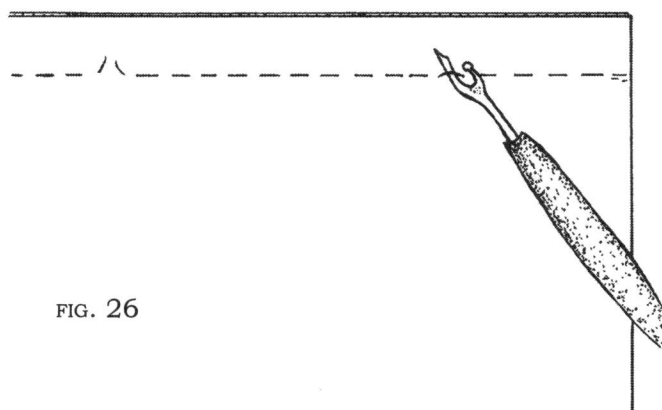

FIG. 26

3. To rip out a certain area, cut a stitch on each side of the stitching that you want to remove. Now pull one of the broken threads and remove the stitching. (If the area you are ripping out is long, you will need to cut the thread in several areas.) If you are not ripping a whole seam, it may be necessary to loosen about 2 inches of thread on either end of the area to be removed so that the replacement thread can be tied on.

"A time to rend, and a time to sew."
Ecclesiastes 3:7

Gathering

Gathers are what give a skirt or ruffle that
full and feminine appearance.

1. To practice making gathers, you will need to cut 2 pieces of fabric. The first is to be 6 inches long and 4 inches wide, and the second 12 inches long and 6 inches wide. For this exercise, we will be working with the long sides of both of these pieces of fabric.

2. Prepare your needle for sewing with a single thread (20 inches long for each row); then stitch two rows of running stitches along the 12-inch side of the larger piece of fabric. Make the first row $^1/_2$ inch from the edge and the second $^1/_4$ inch from the edge. (See fig. 27.) *Leave a 4-inch tail of thread on each end.* (If you are using a machine, set the stitch length to the longest setting but leave the same length tails.)

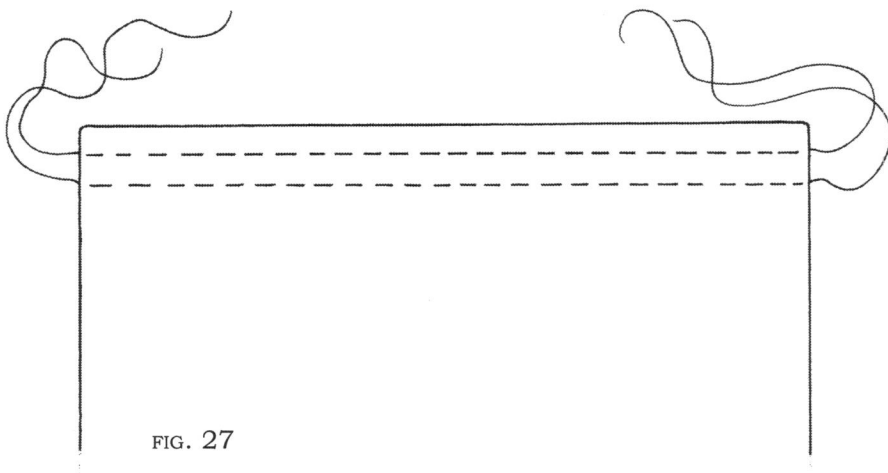

FIG. 27

3. Now, fold the stitched piece in half to find the center and mark the center point with a pin. Next, find the center on the shorter, non-stitched piece and pin the centers to each other with right sides together. Keeping the *raw edges* even, match up the ends and pin. (See fig. 28.)

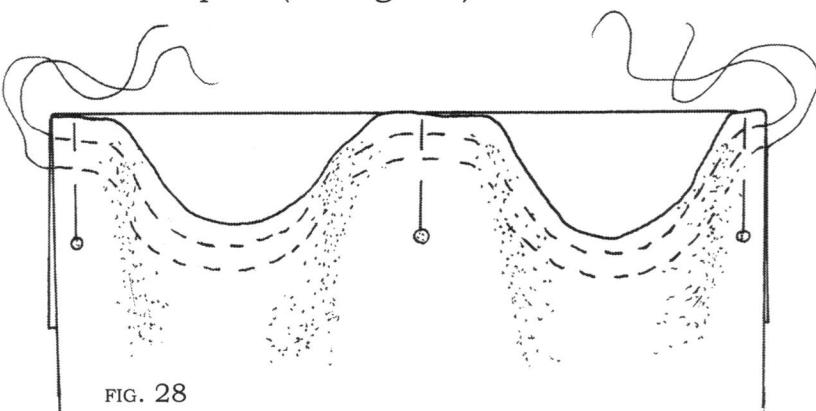

FIG. 28

4. Begin to gather the fabric by gently pulling the two threads together and sliding the fabric down the thread. (If you are using a machine, pull the *bobbin thread*.) Be very careful not to pull out the threads completely or break the threads! When you have gathered up one side—it should be the same length as the nongathered piece it is pinned to—wrap the thread tails around the end pin to secure them. Pin the gathered fabric to the nongathered fabric in a few more places. (See fig. 29.)

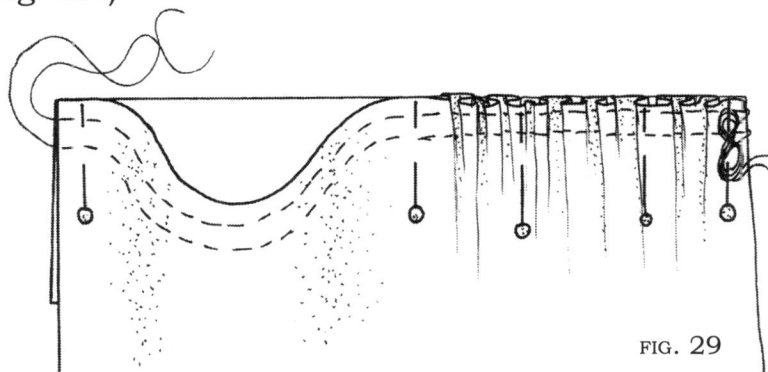

FIG. 29

5. Now gather the other side in the same way; then secure the threads by wrapping them around the pin at the end.

6. If you are sewing with a machine, use a regular length stitch and sew across the gathers using a $1/2$-inch seam allowance. Stitch just below the *lower row* of gathering stitches. (See fig. 30.) It is not necessary to remove the pins, *but be careful!* "Walk" the needle slowly over each pin (See "Sewing with a Machine" on page 29.). If you are sewing by hand, you will need to backstitch the whole length of the gathers to give it strength.

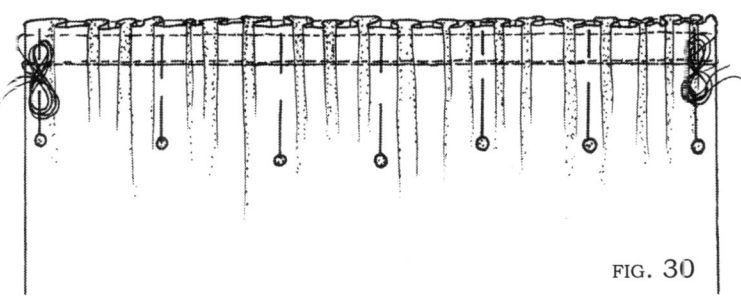

FIG. 30

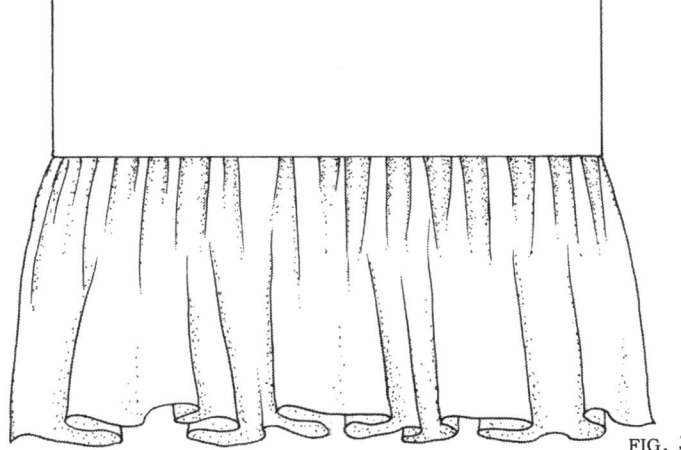

FIG. 31

7. Now you can remove the pins and trim the thread tails. Turn the fabric over so that the right side is facing out and admire your gathers! (See fig. 31.)

The Hope Chest

All throughout history, young ladies have prepared for the vocation of marriage by collecting the items for future use in a home of their own. The French called this collection a trousseau, which translates "clothing bundle," though the trousseau also contained many other things, such as household linens, china, and silverware. In England it was referred to as the *bottom drawer* or the *marriage chest*; and in America, young ladies "hoping" for marriage called them *hope chests*.

In some cultures, the moment a baby girl was born her parents purchased a hope chest and began making and collecting items for it. In others, the chest was given to a girl around age eleven or twelve so that she might start sewing items and storing them away for her future home.

Ideally, by the time of a young lady's marriage, the hope chest would contain everything needed to begin running a household. The list of items would include several quilts, sheets, pillowcases and towels embroidered with handmade lace, tablecloths, napkins, aprons, and numerous crocheted doilies. In her hope chest you would also find a set of china, cookware, silverware, and the always necessary teapot.

The lovely tradition of the hope chest is still practiced today, though not on the scale it was one hundred years ago. Yes, God will call many girls to the beautiful vocation of Religious life; yet still more will be called to the equally noble vocation of wife and mother. The hope chest is a way for young ladies to prepare for their future home in a practical way while praying for their future spouse.

It is important to note that you don't need an actual chest to start your hope chest. The English used a bottom drawer and in other cultures they used whatever containers were available. Many of the items featured in this book would make lovely additions to a hope chest. The traditional chest contained many kitchen, table, and bed linens (which were not necessarily made of linen). Some things, such as china, vases, or a pretty picture frame, might be found at yard sales and thrift shops. Still other ideas include a good cookbook, a recipe box, or other kitchen helps. A word of warning, however: A beautiful hope chest can become quite cluttered if the collection is not limited to things that are truly special to you.

Saint Maria Goretti,
Patroness of Girls, Pray for Us!

26

Basic Embroidery Stitches

Do not be intimidated by the term *embroidery*. Think of it as simply drawing with thread! In addition to these stitches, the simple backstitch works well for embroidery lines. In order to practice these stitches, you should use an embroidery hoop and 2 strands of *embroidery floss*.

1. Cut an 18-inch length of embroidery floss (or whatever length you are comfortable with). The floss is made up of 6 threads or strands. Carefully separate the strands of floss and thread a needle with two together for this project. (Different effects can be achieved by using more or less strands.) This is where a needle threader will come in very handy! (Only one thread is shown in the following illustrations to make the stitch easier to see.)

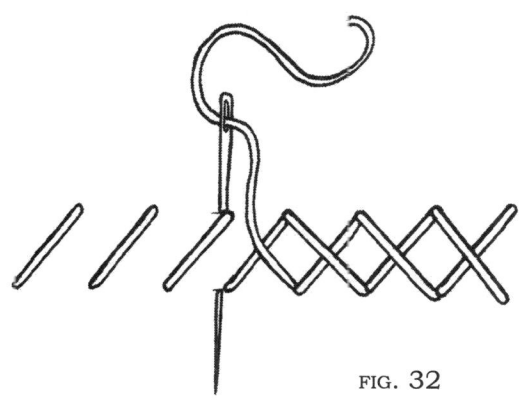

FIG. 32

2. The first stitch is the very easy *cross stitch*. (See fig. 32.) This is the same stitch that is used for "counted cross stitch."

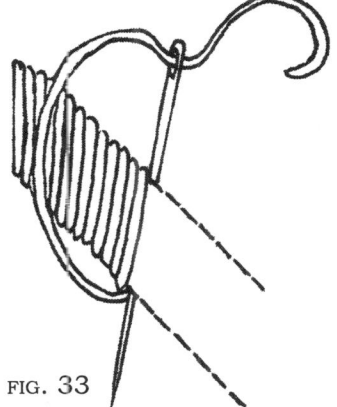

FIG. 33

3. This next stitch, the *satin stitch*, is used for filling in larger areas. One way to use this stitch is to outline the shape in backstitches and then use a satin stitch to fill in. (See fig. 33.)

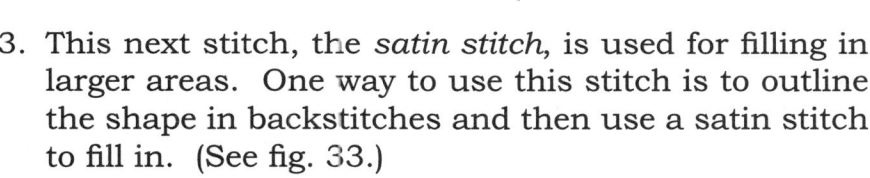

FIG. 34

4. The last stitch is known as a *blanket stitch*. It is useful for trimming a hem or edge as a decorative final touch. (See fig. 34.)

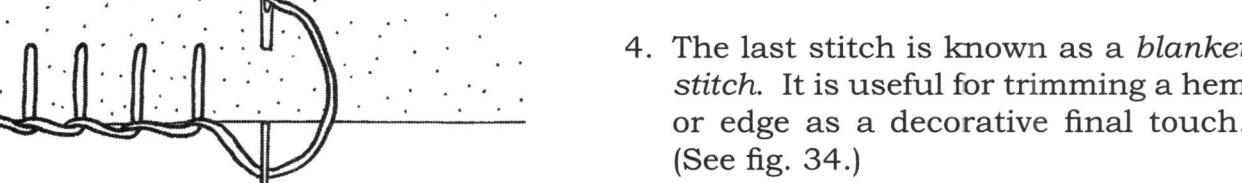

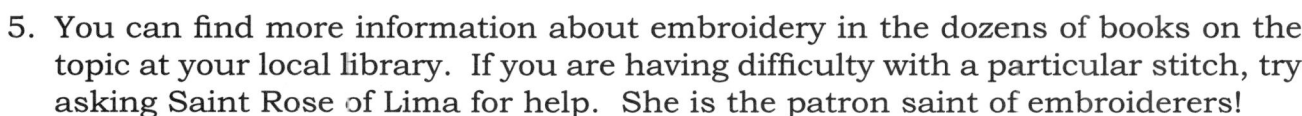

5. You can find more information about embroidery in the dozens of books on the topic at your local library. If you are having difficulty with a particular stitch, try asking Saint Rose of Lima for help. She is the patron saint of embroiderers!

The Sewing Machine

This is the very first sewing machine. It was invented in 1845 by a twenty-six-year-old New Englander named Elias Howe.

This later model from the mid-1890s was called a "high arm" sewing machine. It sold for about $20, including the cabinet.

Sewing with a Machine

It would be impossible to explain in just one lesson all the different functions of all the different types of sewing machines. If there is a sewing machine in your home, chances are there is someone there who can give you basic instruction on how to use it. If you have purchased a new machine, the owner's manual will have all the necessary information in it. Here are a few helpful tips and hints to get you started:

- Practice first! It may take a little while to get accustomed to sewing with a machine. Practice on a large scrap of cloth before attempting a project.

- A good way to get used to the feel of the machine is to practice sewing on paper. To do this, unthread the machine, both top and bobbin. Next, with a pencil, draw both curved and straight lines on a sheet of paper. Now, simply sew along the lines! When you are done, you can hold the paper up to the light and see how well you stayed on the lines.

- If the machine seems too fast for you at first, you can slow things down a bit: Take a clean dry sponge; cut a piece about 2 by 3 inches and position it under the foot pedal so that the pedal cannot be pushed down all the way. Use masking tape to hold the sponge in place. Adjust the size of your piece of sponge to fit your needs—you may need one that is larger or smaller.

- When it is necessary to sew over pins, such as when sewing gathers, do not use the pedal but instead turn the side wheel by hand to *slowly* "walk" the needle over the pins.

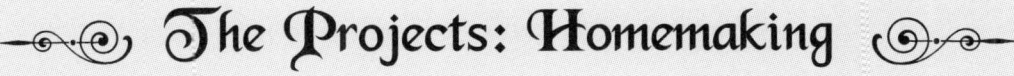

The Projects: Homemaking

Even though these projects are listed in a **Homemaking** category, *most* of these projects make wonderful gifts for friends and family members.

Each project is labeled with a number to indicate the difficulty level: 1—Beginner; 2—Intermediate; 3—Advanced.

Homemaking is the act of taking care of the home and making it a place where people enjoy being. Though a wife and mother is usually referred to as a "homemaker," the skills necessary for this job can be practiced at any age. Making a house into a home is something *everyone* can be part of!

Saint Monica, Patroness of Homemakers, Pray for Us!

Choosing and Preparing Fabric

When choosing fabrics, don't forget to check your scrap box,
especially if the project is small and doesn't require much material.
If you are purchasing new fabric, we recommend *natural fibers* and
blends of natural fibers and synthetic since they will work best in the
projects outlined in this book.

A *natural fiber* fabric is one that
comes from nature such as cotton,
wool, linen, or silk. (Rayon is derived
from natural sources, but is man-
made.) Sometimes these natural
fibers are blended with a synthetic
(man-made) fiber to improve certain
qualities of the fiber. For example,
polyester is often blended with cotton
to make the final fabric less prone to
wrinkles. For all the projects in this
book, it is recommended that the
reader avoid knit fabrics.

If you are making a washable item,
such as a cloth napkin, you will need to first wash and dry your fabric prior to
cutting out the pieces for the project. Wash and dry your piece of fabric in the same
manner in which the finished project will be washed and dried. This way the fabric
will shrink *before* all your hard work goes into it. (A dryer will cause more shrinkage
than line drying.) It is also a good idea to press out any wrinkles in your fabric prior
to cutting out the pattern pieces.

When using a pattern to cut pieces for a project, make sure to
place the pattern pieces on the fabric in such a way as to not
waste fabric. If you have a large piece of fabric and a small
pattern piece, always place the pattern as close to the edge of
the fabric as possible. This will leave most of your fabric intact
for a future project.

All the pattern pieces must be placed on the *grain* of the fabric.
The arrows on the pattern <u>must</u> run parallel to the grain of the
fabric. The *selvage* is the name for the tightly woven edges on
the length of the fabric. All the threads run either parallel or
perpendicular to the selvage. Those threads running parallel to
the selvage are called the *"warp"* or the *"lengthwise grain;"* those
running perpendicular to the selvage are called the *"weft"* or the
"crosswise grain."

Sometimes a scrap of fabric no longer has its selvages and it is necessary to find the direction of the grain to determine the placement of the pattern. This process is called putting the fabric *on grain* (parallel to either the lengthwise or crosswise grain) and can be done in one of two ways. The first method is to find a thread at the edge of the fabric and carefully pull it creating a faint line across the fabric. Cutting along this line will produce a straight edge to line the pattern up with. The second way to achieve a straight edge is to make a small cut (about one inch) at one end of the piece of fabric and rip it. Woven fabric will always rip along the straight of the grain. It is *very* important that all pattern pieces be lined up with the grain of the fabric. If they are not, the finished item will not look right and will not hold up to frequent use.

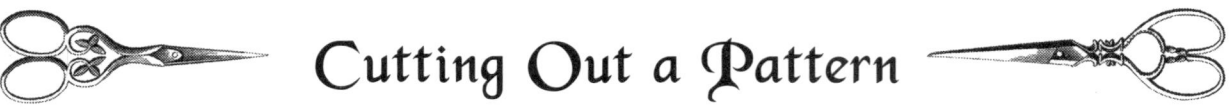

Cutting Out a Pattern

When cutting out a pattern from your chosen fabric, the most important thing is to make sure *the arrows on the pattern piece are running parallel to the grain of the fabric.* Smooth the fabric out on a large flat surface and carefully pin the pattern to it, keeping as close to the edge as possible. Staying close to the edge ensures there will be less wasted fabric. After pinning on the pattern, you are ready to cut around it. When using a very small pattern piece, it is sometimes easier to trace around the piece with a pencil and then cut it out. If a pattern says to place a particular edge "on the fold," simply fold up the edge of your fabric and place the indicated edge of the pattern along the fold of the fabric. Be sure that this folded edge is running *with* the grain of the fabric.

It is a good idea to read all the directions for a project before beginning it!

What Is a Natural Fiber?

The term *natural fiber* is used to describe any thread or cloth that is from natural sources instead of man-made. Human hands, of course, make the thread and cloth, but the origin of the fiber is nature. It is made by God.

Natural fibers have been around for many centuries, long before man figured out how to make polyester and nylon. The first natural fibers recorded in the Bible were the fig leaves Adam and Eve used and the animal skins God Himself fashioned for our fallen parents. For a long time man used the whole skins of animals to cover himself, but, eventually, he learned to harvest the hair or wool from the animals and spin, or twist, it into long threads to be woven into cloth. There are many different natural fibers, but the most popular are wool, cotton, linen, and silk.

Wool yarn or thread is spun from the wool of sheep. There are many different breeds of sheep throughout the world and each breed offers a slightly different wool. Wool is well known for its warmth and water-repelling properties thanks to a natural oil called lanolin in the wool fibers.

Cotton is a lighter and shorter fiber than wool. It is harvested from the cotton plant, but before it can be used the seeds must be removed from the boll of cotton. This was a tedious process done by hand—until Eli Whitney invented the cotton gin in 1793. The invention of this machine greatly increased the availability and popularity of cotton.

Historians date the use of linen as far back as 8000 B.C. Linen is made from the stalks of the flax plant. The process for getting the linen fibers from the little flax plant is a long one that involves several steps—sometimes it takes as many as three weeks from harvest to spinning. Linen cloth is cool and strong.

Silk is made from the cocoons of the silkworm. These little worms are raised on a diet of mulberry leaves; after they spin their cocoons, they become moths and leave their cocoons. The long strand of silk that makes up the cocoon is carefully unwound and twisted with three to ten others to make one silk thread. Silk producers estimate that one cocoon produces a strand approximately 600 yards long, but it takes almost 700 cocoons to make one silk shirt!

Pincushion

A fun and useful project to make for yourself or a friend.

To make the pincushion you will need the following:

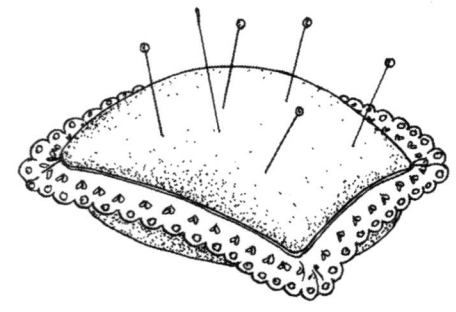

- 2 squares of a tightly woven fabric. Avoid light-weight fabrics. Upholstery-type fabrics work quite well. If you are purchasing new fabric, you will need to ask for $^3/_8$th of a yard.

- Fiberfill. (This is sold in craft or discount stores and is used to stuff everything from stuffed animals to pillows. You will find many uses for your leftovers. ☺)

- Optional: $^1/_2$ yard (18 inches) of $^1/_2$ inch wide lace of your choice.

- Optional: A tiny ribbon rose or silk-ribbon bow. These can be found in the sewing section of your local craft or discount stores.

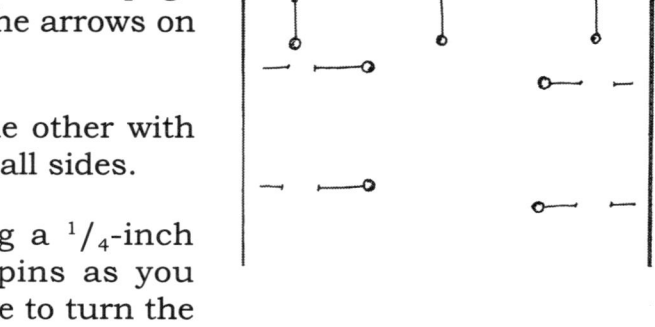

1. Lay your fabric out on a clean, flat surface such as a tabletop. Using the "Pincushion" pattern on page 91, align the grain of the fabric with the arrows on the pattern piece and cut 2 squares.

2. Stack the 2 squares one on top of the other with *right sides* together. Place pins along all sides.

3. Now stitch around the edge, leaving a $^1/_4$-inch seam allowance and removing the pins as you come to them. So that you will be able to turn the pincushion over and stuff it, leave an area without stitching. To do this, begin stitching $1^1/_4$ inch from one of the corners and finish stitching $1^1/_4$ inch from the corner next to it. This will leave you a 2-inch opening along one side. (See illustration at left.)

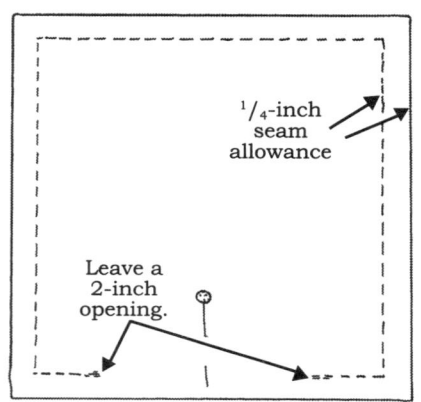

$^1/_4$-inch seam allowance

Leave a 2-inch opening.

If you are hand sewing your pincushion, stitch the seams with a backstitch for added strength; don't forget to make good knots at the stopping and starting points.

4. Remove the last pin and turn the pincushion right side out. Very carefully, use an ink pen with its pointed cap *on* to push out the corners.

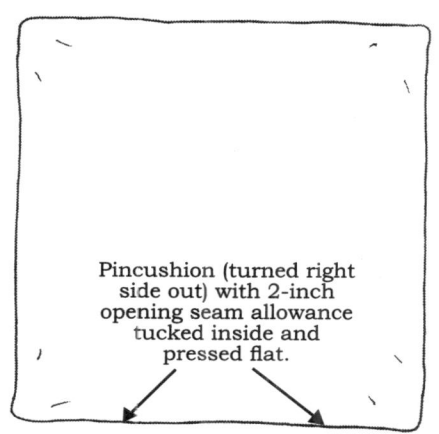

Pincushion (turned right side out) with 2-inch opening seam allowance tucked inside and pressed flat.

5. Now press well with a warm iron. Make sure when ironing that the seam allowance on the 2-inch section that was left open is tucked inside.

6. It is now time to stuff! A pincushion must be stuffed very tight—so that the pins and needles stay where they are put. This is why we recommend that you use a strong backstitch when hand sewing. Use the same pen with the cap to help you push the Fiberfill far into each corner. Use small handfuls of the Fiberfill at a time—this is much easier than trying to shove a huge amount into the small opening at one time.

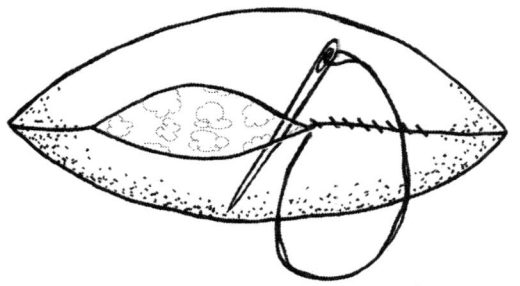

7. When the pincushion is as full as you can get it, carefully stitch the opening closed using a *slip stitch* as shown in the illustration. To do this, bring the needle through the fabric on both sides of the opening, staying as close as possible to the folded edge of the fabric. Keep your stitches small and close together. For stitching up this opening, a double thread will be stronger than a single.

8. For those who would like a fancier cushion: Affix lace by using a single thread and the same stitch used to close the hole. To begin, attach the lace by stitching the edge of the lace to the seam. If you are using a flat lace, you will need to make a little pleat at the corners so that the lace will go around the corner without being pulled too tight. To do this, simply stop your stitching at the center of the corner and tuck about $1/4$ inch of the unsewn lace under the spot you have just sewn. Go back a few stitches and catch in all the layers as you secure the pleat to the corner. It is not necessary to add this

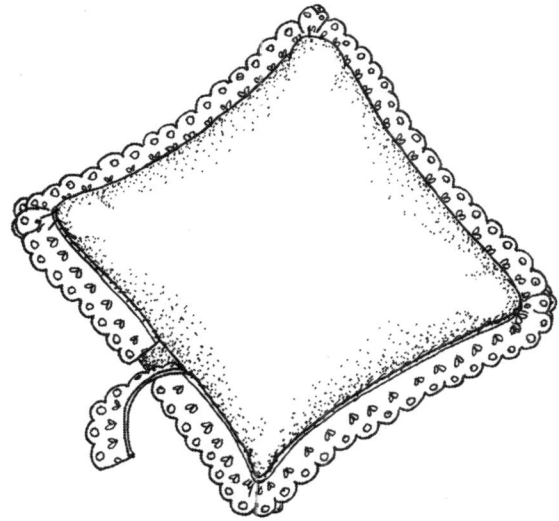

fullness when using gathered lace. When you've come all the way around, overlap the ends of the lace $1/2$ inch for a neat finish.

And that completes your pincushion! If you would like, you can further decorate it by adding a tiny ribbon rose or silk-ribbon bow to the top of it. It's up to you! These make wonderful gifts for sewing friends.

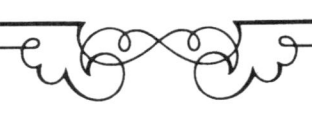

Did You Know?

The Thimble

The word "thimble" is a contraction of the words "thumb" and "bell." When the thimble was first introduced in the seventeenth century, it was worn on the thumb. Now the "correct" position is on the middle finger.

Lady's Companion

A "Lady's Companion" was a small sewing case that a lady would carry with her when she went to her sewing circle gatherings. The little box was made of leather or wood and usually had the words *"Lady's Companion"* painted on it. Popular during the late eighteenth century and all through the nineteenth century, this sewing companion contained everything a lady needed for sewing.

A stitch in time?

Do you know what the old saying "A stitch in time saves nine" means? It means if you mend a rip, tear, or hole when it is small, you will have much less work than if you wait until it gets larger. A stitch *now* will prevent you from having to make *nine* later!

A washerwoman in the mid 1800s made about $11.00 per month.

Needle Book

This project is more of a craft than a sewing project, but this is such a useful little item that we wanted to include it. A needle book is a wonderful way to carry your favorite needles to your sewing circle gatherings or quilting bees.

To make this needle book, you will need the following:

- Two 3 X 5 index cards.

- 5-inch by 7-inch piece of light-weight cotton fabric.

- 17 inches of $1/4$-inch wide ribbon.

- A 3 X 5 piece of felt in any color you like.

- Glue. (Any white or *tacky* craft glue will work.)

- 4 clothespins are optional. (These will be your "extra hands" to help hold your work.)

1. Take one of the 3 X 5 index cards; carefully fold it in half and then open it up again to form a crease down the center.

2. Lay the 5 X 7 piece of fabric on a flat work surface with the *right side* face down. Now place the creased 3 X 5 card in the center of the fabric and spread a bead of glue all around the outer edges of the card.

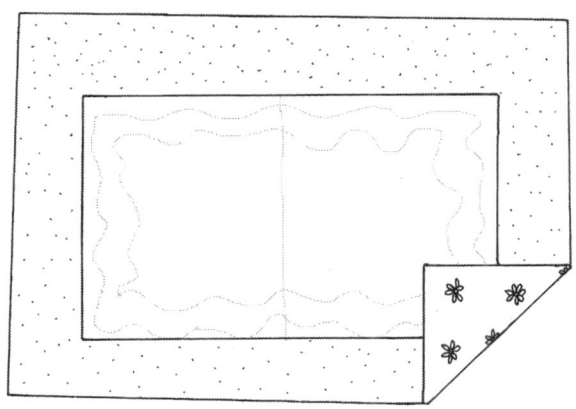

3. Carefully fold the fabric over the edges of the card, beginning with the corners.

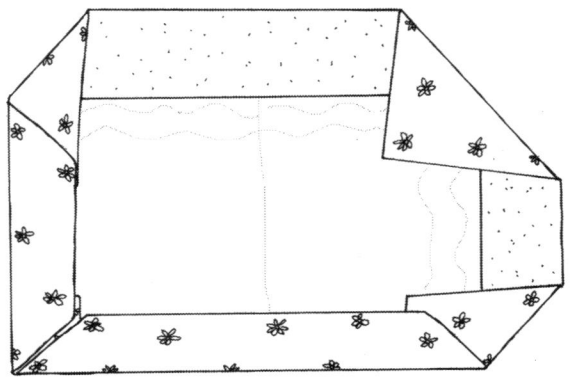

4. After the corners have been folded, fold each side in (add a little glue to the corners if necessary). Use your "extra hands"—the clothespins—if you need them.

5. Now take the other 3 X 5 index card; using a ruler, draw a line around the inside border, inset $1/4$ inch from the edge. Cut on this line, but set aside the $1/4$ inch that you cut off. You will need some of it later.

6. Take the index card you have just trimmed and use it as a pattern for the felt. Trace around it on the felt and cut out the felt piece. Set it aside.

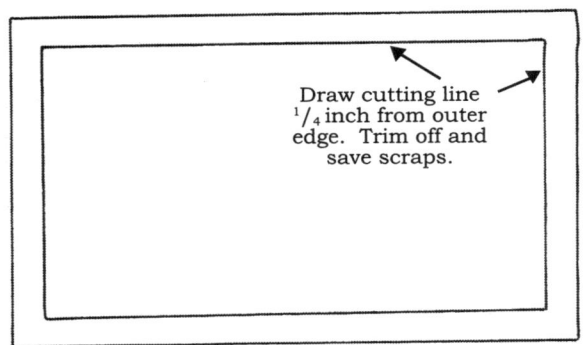

Draw cutting line $1/4$ inch from outer edge. Trim off and save scraps.

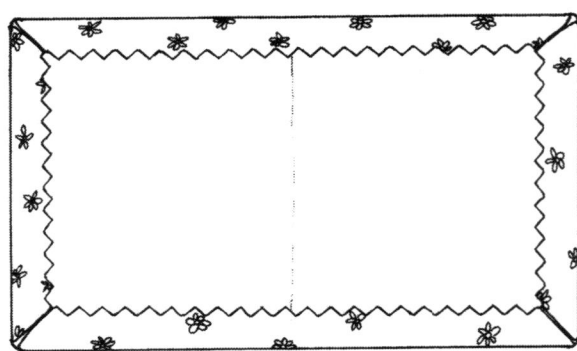

7. At this point, if you like, trim the edge of the card with a pair of decorative scissors such as *pinking shears*. Pinking shears will create a zigzag effect.

8. Now fold the smaller card in half; then open it back up to form a crease. Apply glue to the lined side of the card and carefully place it on top of the fabric-covered card. Allow this to dry for several hours (or overnight) with the clothespins holding the corners.

9. When the glue is completely dry, take the piece of felt that you cut in step 6 and center it on the index card side of the needle book. Then place the whole book in the center of the ribbon and use the clothespins to hold everything in place. Stitch down the center, sewing a few extra stitches as necessary to secure the ribbon at the "binding" too. *Be very careful* when pushing the needle through all the layers. Use a thimble if necessary.

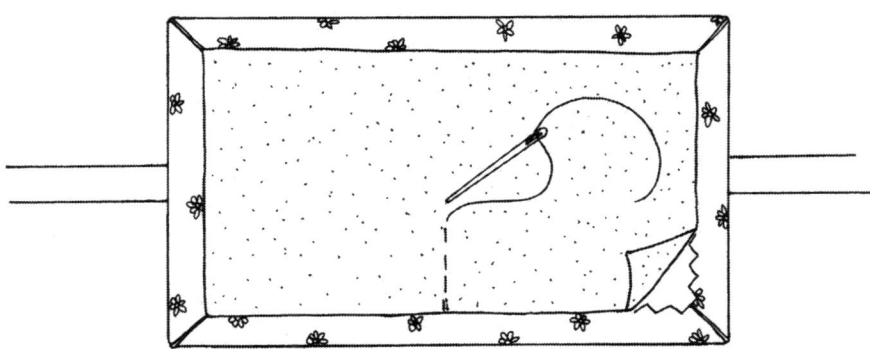

10. After stitching your needle book, you can add a holder for a needle threader. Cut a $1^1/_4$ inch long piece from the index card trim you cut. Place a small drop of glue on each end of the $1^1/_4$-inch piece and place it in the center of the inside front cover of the book. When dry, slide in your favorite needle threader!

Pretty Hand Towel

Exactly how these towels turn out depends entirely upon your choice of trims. Terry cloth, woven cotton, or linen all work equally well. Take your towel to the store with you when choosing trims.

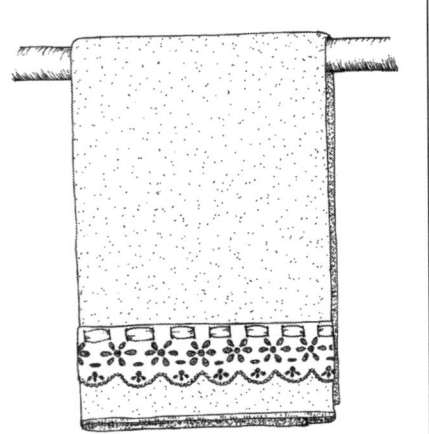

To make a pretty hand towel,
you will need the following:

- $^1/_2$ yard of lace or *eyelet*. Either flat or ruffled is fine.

- $^1/_2$ yard of ribbon that is $^1/_4$ to $^3/_8$ inch wide. Your choice of ribbon will depend on your choice of lace.

- A hand towel

1. The first step in this project is to select the towel you will use. Be sure to wash and dry the towel before adding any trims.

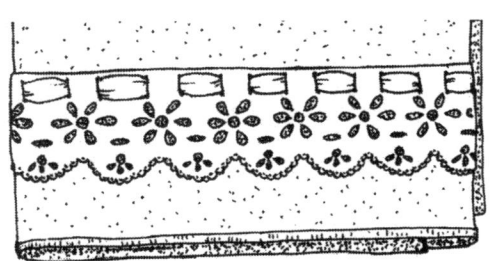

2. The next step is to choose the trim. Bring the towel with you when shopping for the trim; lay the lace across the towel to get an idea of how it will look after it has been sewn on. Some lace has larger holes at the top and narrow ribbon can be woven in and out of these holes for a pretty effect. Others such as eyelet are gathered and may not even need the addition of a ribbon. For flat lace that a ribbon cannot be woven through, you can stitch the ribbon down along the line where the lace and towel meet to dress up your trim.

3. When pinning the lace or eyelet in place, tuck the ends of the lace under about $^1/_2$ inch on the ends instead of wrapping them around to the back. This will give your trim a neater appearance overall when finished.

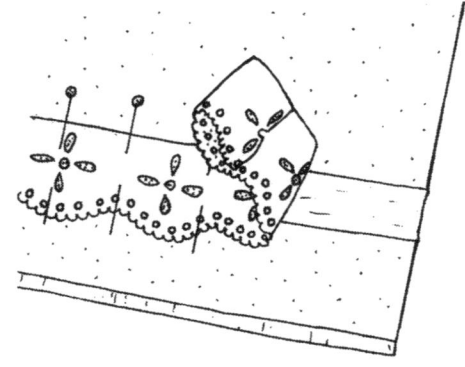

4. The exact position of the lace is not crucial. However, if a terry cloth towel has a line of non-terry fabric toward the bottom, the lace should be positioned over it. Use a neat running stitch to attach the trim, stitching along the top of the lace. (Or straight stitch if using a machine.)

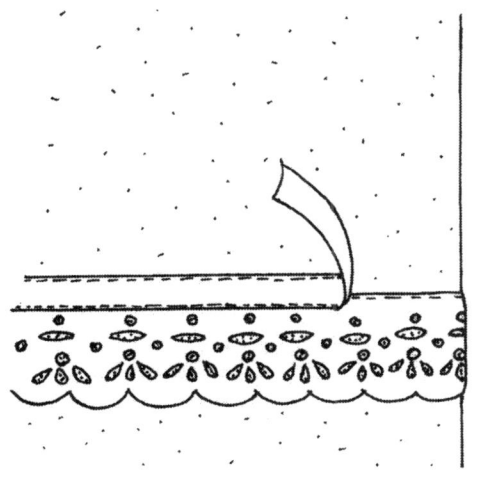

5. If you are planning to sew on ribbon along the line where the lace ends and the fabric begins, basting the lace to the towel is all that is needed at first. This will hold the lace in place while you attach the ribbon with a running stitch on the top and bottom of the ribbon. Don't forget to tuck the ends of the ribbon under instead of wrapping them to the back.

These pretty hand towels look lovely in a bathroom beside the sink or on a bedside table.

Diligence

A pocket handkerchief to hem—
Oh dear, oh dear, oh dear!
How many stitches it will take
Before it's done, I fear.

You set a stitch and then a stitch,
And stitch and stitch away,
Till stitch by stitch the hem is done
And after work is play!

—Christina Rossetti

·~·⊙⎰ Cloth Napkins ⎱⊙·~·

Cloth napkins can be made in a variety of sizes—from 12 to 16 inches. Their edges can also be finished in any number of ways. If you are using a machine, and your napkins will be for practical everyday use, you might consider simply zigzagging the raw edges with a tight zigzag stitch. If your napkins will be for a special function such as a tea party, or if they will be a gift, you will probably want a neater finish such as the one described below. *Please* get help from an adult if you are not accustomed to using an iron.

To make a set of four 14-inch napkins, you will need:

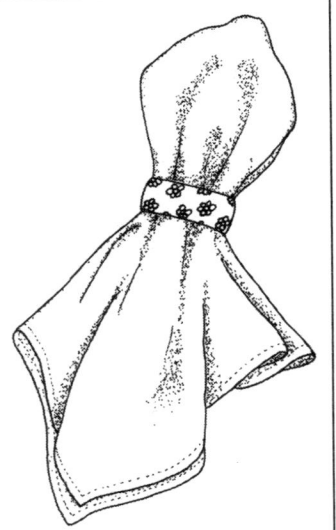

- $^1/_2$ yard of fabric, washed and dried. (Any light- to medium-weight fabric will work. Broadcloth, linen, or a pretty cotton print are some options.)

- Matching thread.

- A 15 by 15-inch square of paper to use as a pattern. Any paper—from tissue paper to an old paper bag—will work.

Fun ideas for napkin rings can be found at the end of the instructions!

1. Make sure your fabric is on grain. (See "Choosing and Preparing Fabric" on page 33 for directions on how to get the fabric on grain.) Cut 4 squares using your pattern.

2. Carefully press a $^1/_4$-inch hem on all sides, turning the hem in toward the wrong side of the fabric. Let the fabric cool; then gently unfold. Using as a guide the point where the pressing lines intersect, trim off the corners of the square. (This extra fabric would make the *mitered* corners too bulky.)

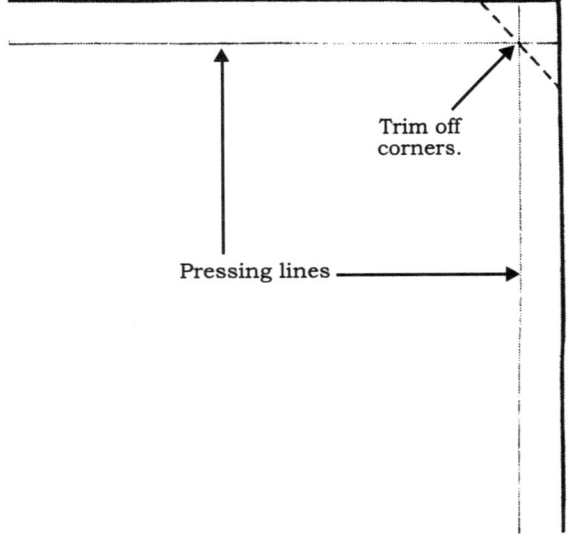

Trim off corners.

Pressing lines

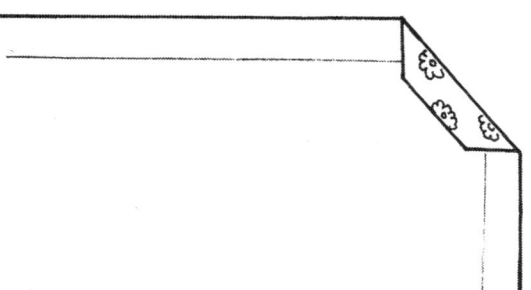

3. After trimming the corners, press this new corner edge in $1/4$ inch; then re-press the edges again to create the hem.

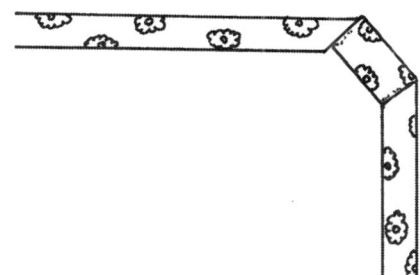

4. Now, turn in all edges $1/4$ inch for the final press. The mitered corners of the napkin should now form a neat point. Then stitch the folded edges down by machine or by hand. If sewing by hand, a running stitch or a hemstitch is fine.

If you are giving your cloth napkins as a gift, fold your set of 4 neatly and tie them with a pretty bow! If you are going to use your new napkins for a special tea party, you might want to dress them up with some of the ideas below!

Napkin Rings

For a *very* easy set of rings, cut 1 inch wide "rings" from bathroom tissue tubes. These can be decorated with paint, markers, or contact paper. You can also glue on shells, buttons, beads, potpourri, or anything else you think of!

Another idea is to use the little bunches of wired, silk flowers from craft stores. Simply twist a few stems together and, if desired, wrap the stems with floral tape. Now just shape the stems into a ring. A little ring of roses would be great for a tea in May in honor of the Blessed Mother!

For a feminine touch, place a pretty ribbon around a napkin and tie it into a bow. A real or silk flower can also be slipped under this napkin ring. Green, red, and white ribbons with a sprig of holly would be a nice touch for a Saint Lucy tea in December.

Just look around your home. There are probably many other things you already have that would make lovely napkin rings!

⊸•⊙⊙ Eyelet Pillowcase ⊙⊙•⊷

This pillowcase will add a feminine touch to your
bedroom or that of a friend.

To make the eyelet pillowcase, you will need the following:

- 1 $^1/_4$ yards of eyelet fabric. These
  fabrics have one end that is finished
  with an eyelet design. They usually
  come in white or cream, which
  gives them a delicate, old-fashioned
  look.

- Thread to match.

Don't forget to wash and dry your
fabric before you begin!

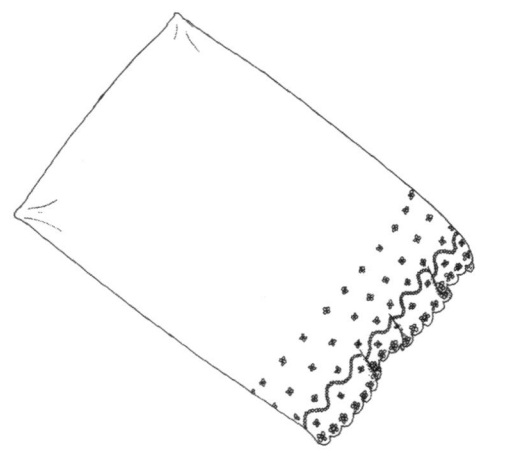

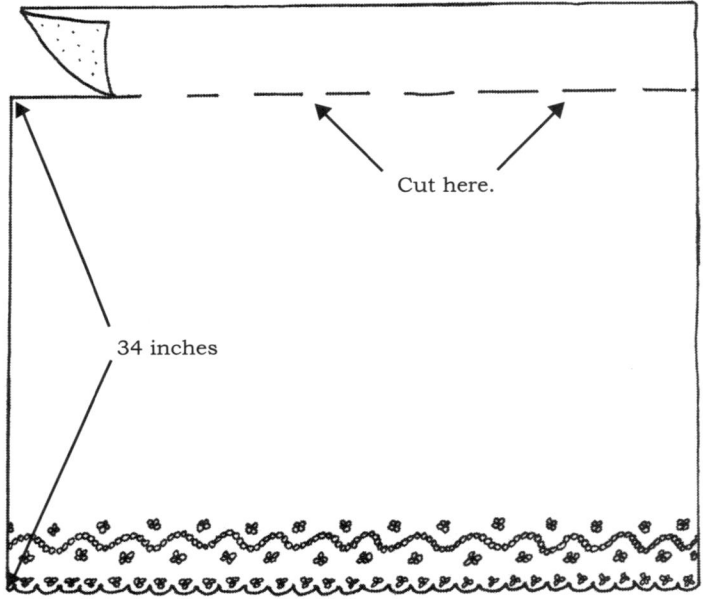

Cut here.

34 inches

1. First, measure from the eyelet
   edge up 34 inches. Cut across
   the fabric at 34 inches. To
   ensure that you cut a straight
   line, mark both ends of the
   fabric. You can also make a
   small cut at the 34-inch line
   and *tear* the fabric.

2. Now, fold the fabric in half lengthwise with right sides together. Using a $1/2$-inch seam allowance, stitch the bottom and then the side of the pillowcase.

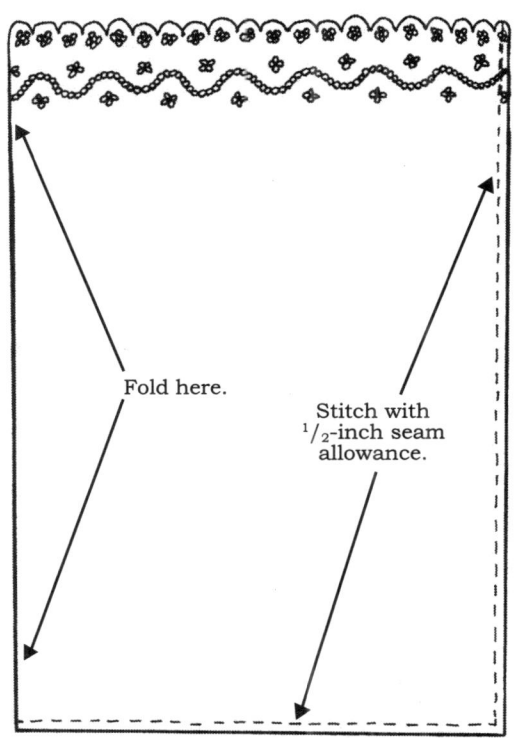

Fold here.

Stitch with $1/2$-inch seam allowance.

3. It is a good idea to finish the seams in your pillowcase because it will be washed many times and unfinished seams will fray a great deal more than finished ones. There are many different ways to finish a seam, but here we will cover the two most basic: the whip stitch, or overcast, and the zigzag.

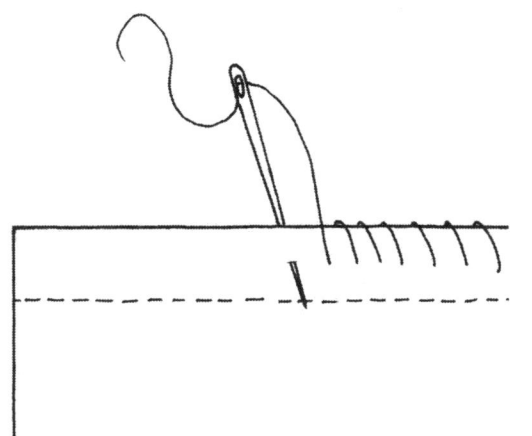

4. If you are hand sewing your pillowcase, you will need to *whip stitch* the seam allowance to finish it. (See instructions on page 19.) This is an easy stitch that will bind the two seam allowances together and cut down on fraying.

5. If you are machine sewing, a simple zigzag stitch will finish your seams neatly and quickly.

6. For a neat, professional finish, turn your pillowcase right side out and press.

Pot Holder

𝒯hese pot holders are both pretty *and* functional! Make some to use now and a few to put away in your hope chest.

To make a pot holder, you will need the following:

- $1/4$ yard medium-weight cotton fabric, washed and dried. Cotton will not melt like some synthetic fabrics will.

- Package of *extra wide double-fold bias tape*. Choose either a contrasting or coordinating color.

- Insulation. You can use storebought *batting*, but an old piece of blanket or an old dish towel will work much better. This insulation is what will be sandwiched in between the two pieces of fabric.

1. Cut 2 squares of your cotton fabric using the "Pot Holder" pattern on page 48. Use the same pattern to cut out the insulation. If you are using a piece of an old blanket or an old terry cloth towel, one piece will be enough. Flannel also works well as an insulator, but you will need at least 3 layers to provide adequate protection from the hot pans.

2. Layer your squares: the cotton squares on the top and bottom and the insulation material in the middle. Make sure that the right sides of the cotton are out. Pin all the layers in place. Baste all around the edge with long basting stitches about $1/4$ inch from the edge.

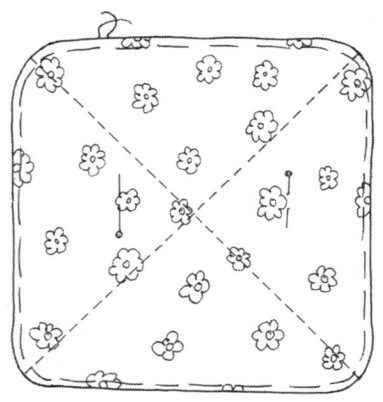

3. Now stitch through all the layers, working from corner to corner. This stitching will hold all the layers in place. If you would like to add extra stitching or place your stitches differently, go right ahead and be creative! Just make sure you make enough stitches to keep the layers from shifting.

4. Cut a piece of extra wide, double-fold bias tape 36 inches long. Unfold it and pin the tape to the pot holder with right sides together and raw edges even. Start pinning it at the top of one of the corners so that you will end at a corner and can place the loop there. Be careful not to stretch the bias tape as you pin it. Stitch along the first $^1/_2$-inch crease.

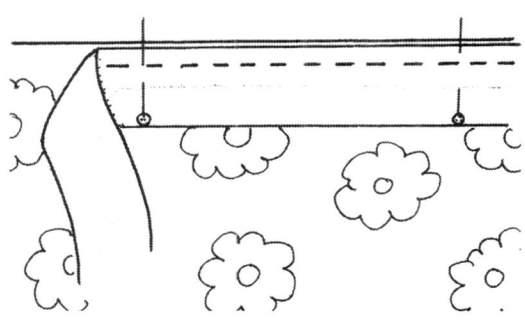

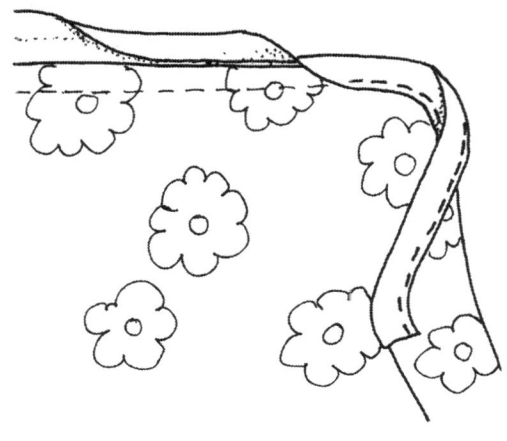

5. Next, fold the bias strip over to enclose the seam allowance; then stitch down. If you are using a machine, you can *carefully* straight stitch through all the layers; but if you are sewing by hand, you may want to catch the fabric in a small *blind stitch* so you don't have to push the needle through all those layers. You can remove those first basting stitches now if they show.

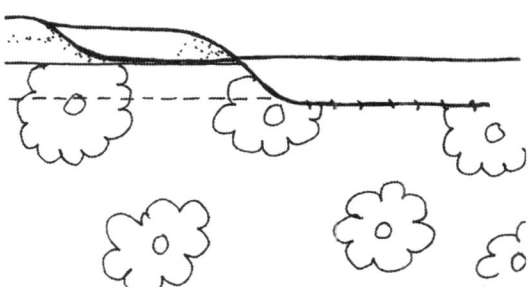

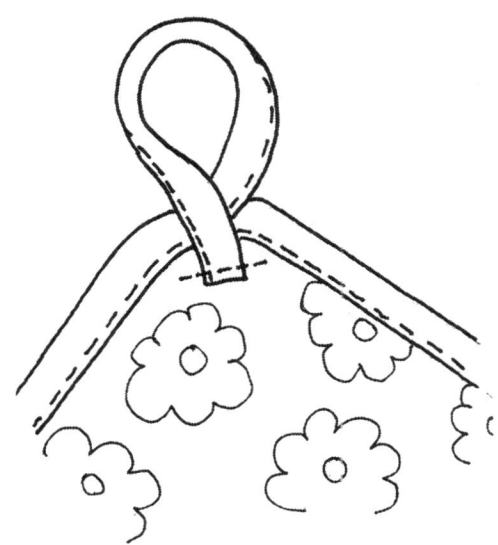

6. After sewing all the way around the pot holder, carefully overlap the first inch of bias trim that was stitched down. To form a loop, stitch closed the "tail" of trim that has been left hanging. Now simply form a loop and attach the tail to the back of the pot holder. For a neater look, tuck the very end of the bias strip under before stitching down to hide the raw edge.

A Bit about the Humble Apron

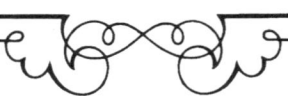

Use of the apron dates back to Biblical times, but it was not until the early 1700s that women began to use them frequently. Until this time, it was usually men who wore aprons to protect their clothes while they worked.

The aprons of this time were made from a rectangle of cloth that was secured at the waist with a belt or the traditional ties. This design, a "half apron," may have been simple, but its uses were many. It kept the woman's clothing clean, of course, but it also worked well when she hauled produce in from the garden and served as a handy polishing cloth.

The "pinned apron" is another type. It had a bib that was attached to the bodice of the lady's dress with carefully placed pins. This style, however, was tedious and time-consuming to put on and take off, so it has all but died out.

The traditional "full apron" is a very practical style. It provides the wearer complete coverage of her clothing and is also easy to use. It usually ties in the back and has straps that go over the shoulders or sometimes around the neck.

Though many country and frontier women had aprons made from practical calico and "homespun," most aprons for ladies were white. These white linen or cotton aprons were sometimes embellished with lovely embroidery and lacework. The women of this time were proud of their position as keepers of the home, and these aprons were beautiful symbols of the place they held.

Around the time of the Great Depression ladies began using fabrics other than the traditional white to make their aprons. They used what they had, such as feed and flour sacks since there was little money to buy new fabric.

Aprons have been worn by children for as long as they have been worn by adults. A little girl's apron, a "pinafore" or "smock," was made to completely cover her dress; it fastened in the back with ties or a button and many times did not have a full gathered skirt, which would get in the way during play. Laundry was not washed as often as it is today, and a pinafore kept the small child's dress clean so that it could be worn for several days.

As a girl grew older, her aprons began to look more like her mother's. Since the girl's help was needed around the house, her apron needed both to protect her dress and to assist her in household duties.

Aprons may not be as popular today as they once were, but they are every bit as practical. Having a few good aprons will go a long way in aiding you in your household chores and will minimize the stains your clothes get. Last but not least, a pretty apron helps to remind us of the beauty and blessings in homemaking.

Saint Martha, Patroness of Homemakers, Pray for Us!

Apron

This apron will fit most anyone from age 7 to 14—or older!
It's great to wear when working in the kitchen or in the
garden, and the generous length of this apron will provide
coverage for the longest of skirts and dresses.

To make the apron, you will need the following:

- 1 yard for sizes 7-10 or $1^1/_4$ yard for sizes 12-14
  of any pretty, 45 inch wide fabric. Keep in mind
  that prints will hide stains better than solids. If
  you would like to add an optional pocket or two
  in matching fabric, add $^1/_4$ yard to the amount
  of fabric you purchase.

- Matching thread

1. After washing and drying the fabric, make sure it is on the straight of the grain
   (See "Choosing and Preparing Fabric" on page 33.) Lay out the fabric on a large
   table top or on the floor and measure 10 inches up from one of the 45-inch sides.
   Cut off this 10 inches. The easiest way to do this is to make a 1-inch snip in the
   fabric at the 10-inch mark and tear it.

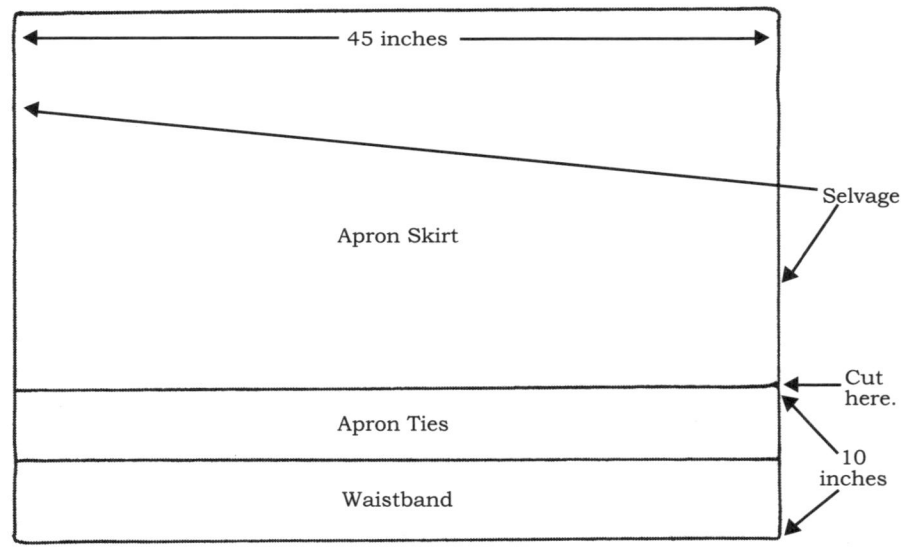

2. This 10 by 45-inch section will be used to make the apron ties and the waistband.
   Next, cut or rip this piece in half lengthwise so that you end up with 2 pieces,
   which are each 5 by 45 inches.

3. Next, measure around your waist using the tape measure. Take one of the 5 by 45-inch strips and cut it to the length of your waist measurement. Take the other strip and cut it exactly in half; set this aside for now.

4. On the waistband piece, measure 5 inches from each end and mark. Set this aside.

5 inches   5 inches

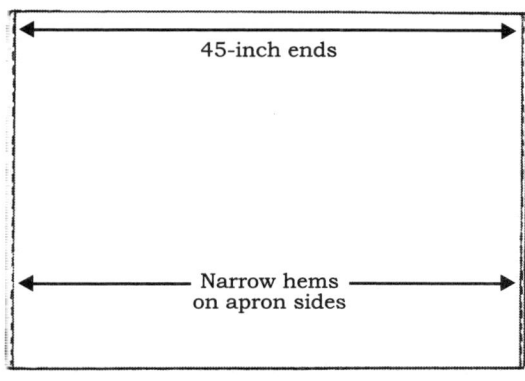

45-inch ends

Narrow hems
on apron sides

5. Now press a narrow hem along each side of the skirt by folding it in $1/4$ inch, pressing, and then folding it over another $1/4$ inch before pressing again. Stitch down these hems.

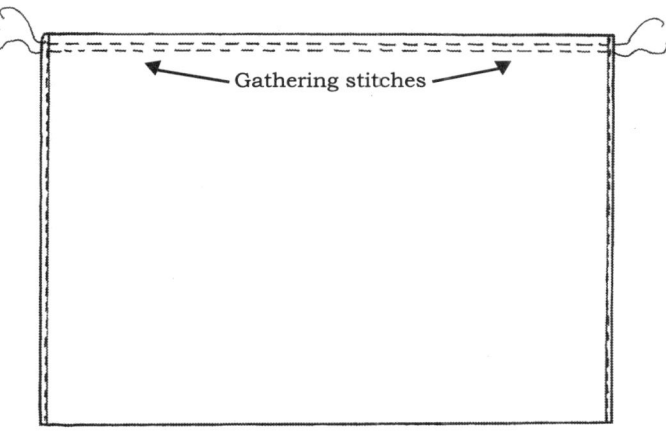

Gathering stitches

6. Run two rows of gathering stitches along the top of the skirt. Make one $1/4$ inch from the edge and the next $1/2$ inch from the edge.

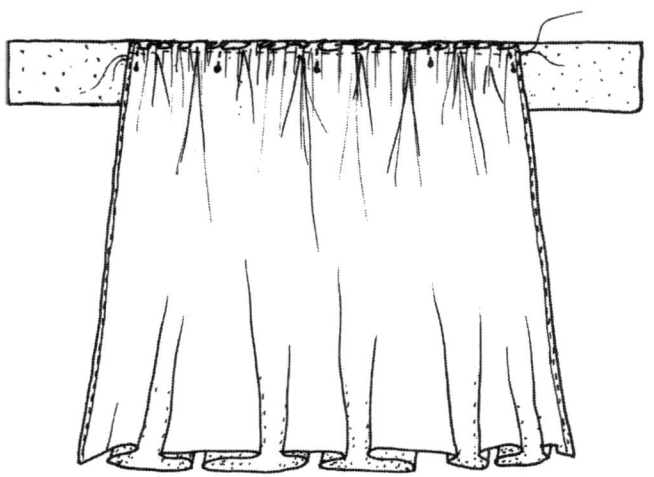

7. Next, find the center of the waistband and the center of the edge to be gathered by folding each in half. Mark the centers. With right sides together, pin hemmed ends of apron to the 5-inch marks on the waistband; then match the center marks and pin. Using your fingers to distribute the gathers evenly, carefully pull gathering stitches and pin them in place. Stitch across the gathers using a $1/2$-inch seam allowance.

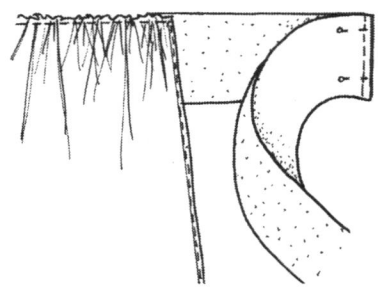

8. Attach the apron ties to the waistband ends. With right sides together, pin ends together and stitch with a $^1/_2$ inch seam allowance. Press the seam allowance open.

9. Now, fold the waistband and ties in half lengthwise, with right sides together; press and then pin. Beginning at the end of one of the ties, stitch across the end at a 45-degree angle and then down the side using a $^1/_4$-inch seam allowance this time. Stop when you come to the point where the skirt is attached. Do the same for the other side.

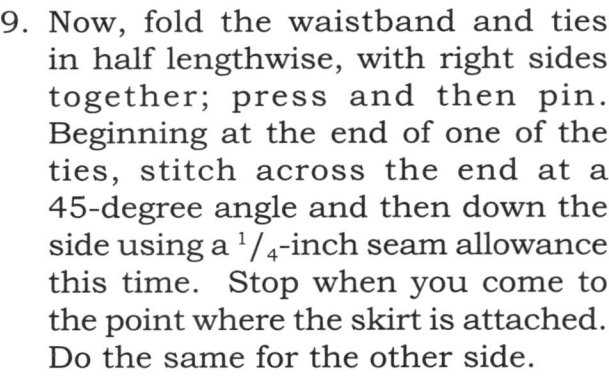

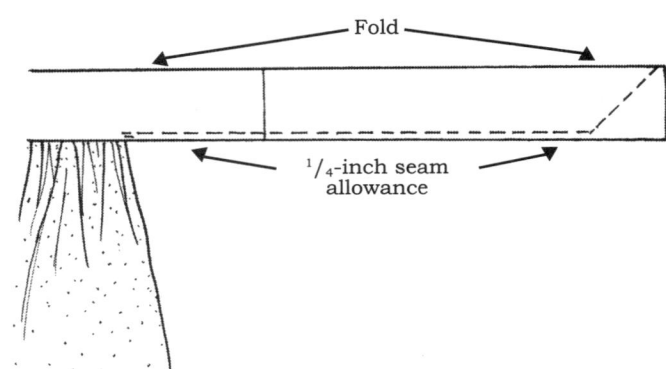

10. Trim away extra fabric in the "triangle" at the end of the apron ties.

11. Turn ties and waistband right side out, using an ink pen with a pointed cap to push out the corners. Press ties and waistband. When pressing, tuck the $^1/_4$-inch seam allowance up and under where the skirt is attached to the waistband.

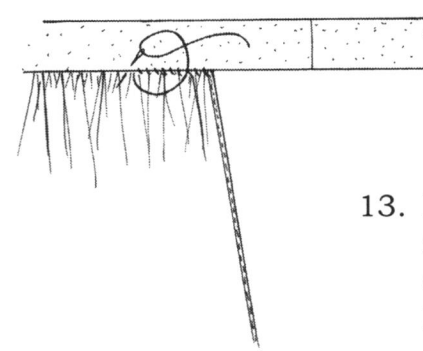

12. Slip stitch the opening closed, encasing the seam allowance.

13. Now, try on your new apron and have someone help you mark the hem. While wearing the apron, stand up straight and tall; then have a helper turn up the hem to the desired length and place a few pins in the hem to hold it. Take off the apron; carefully turn up the fabric evenly along the whole width of the skirt and press in place. Next, fold in some of the turned up fabric to make a neat hem. (See "Hemming" on page 20.) Stitch in place. The hem can be any size but if you need to, you can cut away some of the fabric for a narrower hem.

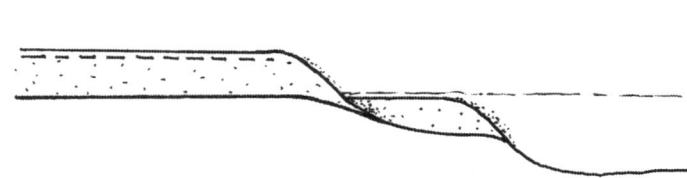

And that completes your apron! You can add many different embellishments to your creation. If you would like to add one or two pockets, see the instructions on the next page.

 # Pockets

To make pockets for your apron you will need one or two 7 by 9-inch pieces of fabric. Matching the fabric to your apron is pretty, but it is also pretty to coordinate fabric. Some examples of a coordinating fabric include a floral apron with checked pockets or a striped apron with solid pockets. The pockets can really be *any* size you like, but for the purpose of these directions, we will use 7 by 9-inch rectangles.

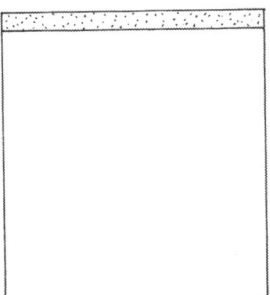

1. First, begin by turning a $^1/_4$-inch hem to the wrong side along one of the short ends of the rectangle. (Follow these directions for *both* rectangles if you are making 2 pockets.) Press well.

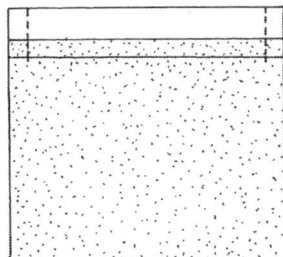

2. Next, flip the pocket over and turn the hemmed edge 1 inch to the *right* side. Press well. Stitch a $^1/_4$-inch seam from the top of the pocket to the edge of the flap on both sides.

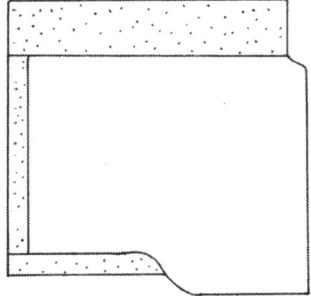

3. Now turn this little flap to the right side and press, making sure that the corners are pushed out completely. Press a $^1/_4$-inch hem on the 3 remaining sides of the pocket.

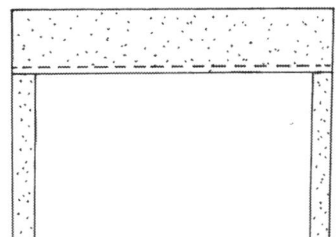

4. Sew a line of *top stitching* across the top of the pocket.

5. Try on your apron again. This time, place your hands in the area that you feel would be a good spot for your pocket(s). Have a helper pin it in place loosely with one pin. Take off the apron and lay it out as flat as possible. Turn the pocket so that its bottom runs parallel to the hem of the apron and its side runs parallel to the side of the apron. (If you are sure you want to include a pocket, it is easier to place it *before* gathering the top of the skirt.) Top stitch the sides and bottom of the pocket about $^1/_8$ inch from the edge of the pocket.

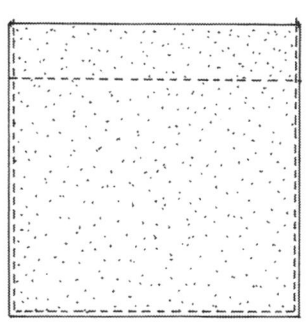

Home Altar Cloths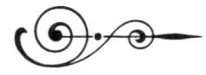

These altar cloths are a great way to celebrate the Church's seasons and feasts in your own home. In her rich tradition and wisdom, the Catholic Church has assigned several different colors to represent different seasons of the Church year and different feasts and Holy days. See the note at the end of the lesson for a list of colors and the times at which to display them.

To make one or more home altar cloths, you will need the following:

- Light- to medium-weight fabric in the color and size you need. To determine the size of your cloth, measure the space on your altar that you would like covered and then add 1 inch in both directions. For example, if you would like the finished altar cloth to be 5 by 7 inches, you will need a 6- by 8-inch piece.

- Thread to match.

- Optional: Embroidery floss and a needle for monogramming.

Do you have a home altar?

An altar can be any place that is set aside to honor Jesus, His Mother, or one of His saints. It can be as small as a corner of a dresser top or a little shelf. Just pick a spot, lay down your cloth, and find an appropriate statue or picture—you have a home altar! If you have room for a tiny vase, you can even add freshly picked wild flowers!

1. To finish the edges of your altar cloth, follow the directions listed for the "Cloth Napkin" project on page 44.

2. After the edges have been hemmed, you can either leave your cloth plain or add an embroidered design to it. The easiest embroidery stitch is the *cross stitch*, which is shown in the illustration above. Lightly pencil in the design and then trace it with stitches using embroidery floss. Even a simple backstitch done in this way looks lovely. Experiment with the gold-colored floss as well as the whites and off whites. Blue stitches on a white cloth are appropriate for Marian feast days.

For many great ideas on what to stitch in order to decorate your altar cloth, check out *Saints, Signs, & Symbols* by W. Ellwood Post. This book is filled with wonderful old symbols, crests, and monograms and will provide much inspiration. Though this is not a stitchery book, you can copy or transfer the simply drawn designs using dressmaker's tracing paper.

Here are a few possibilities for embroidery:

| "Jesus" | "Mary" | "Christ" |

These can be drawn or traced onto the fabric and then embroidered. You can use a simple cross stitch or you can outline them with a backstitch and then fill in with a satin stitch.

Liturgical Colors

White: This color symbolizes joy, innocence, and triumph. It is used on feasts of Our Lord, all feasts of the Blessed Mother, all the saints who were not martyrs, the feasts of angels, and during Christmas and Easter. White may also be used in Masses for the dead.

Red: Red symbolizes fire, royalty, and blood. It is used on the feasts of the martyrs and Apostles (except St. John), Pentecost, Palm Sunday, Good Friday, and on celebrations of Christ's Passion and His Cross.

Green: This color symbolizes life, growth, and hope. It is used during Ordinary Time.

Violet: This color is a symbol of penance, expectation, and purification. It is used during the seasons of Lent and Advent. Violet may also be used in Masses for the dead.

Rose: Rose is used in place of violet on Laetare (fourth Sunday of Lent) and Gaudete (third Sunday of Advent) Sundays.

Black: Black is a symbol of death and may be used in Masses for the dead.

History of Quilting

Quilt making, as we know it, did not become widely popular until the nineteenth century. Before this time most quilts, or "coverlets" as they were called, were made using a whole piece of cloth usually woven by the woman of the house. It was about the 1830s when the Industrial Revolution made its way to the United States and factories began to produce the fabric that once had been so painstakingly spun and woven by hand. Cloth was now more widely available, but it was expensive—not a scrap could be wasted. The wives and mothers of this era saved every piece of fabric, large and small and, out of their frugality, the patchwork quilt was born.

Quilts and quilting became an important part of people's lives. The quilts lovingly stitched at home were loaded onto covered wagons when people started heading West. There they not only covered beds but were also used to cover doors and windows in the new cabin. Before a family left to move "out West," sometimes friends of the lady who was moving would give her a "friendship quilt." This quilt was a collection of blocks, each one pieced and signed by one of her friends. It was a very special reminder of those people in her life whom she might never see again. Once a family was settled in their new western home, the women would often include a scrap from something they were sewing in a letter to those "back home."

VARIABLE STAR

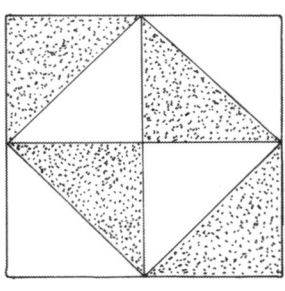

BROKEN DISHES

Although this practice might seem strange to us, it was very common for women to exchange scraps. In this way a woman could include many different colors and prints in her quilt without having to buy very many different fabrics. Unmarried young ladies who were making quilts for their hope chests got together and traded scraps with their friends so that everyone had a beautiful variety. One tradition said that a lady must have *twelve* quilts in her hope chest before she married. That is a lot of scraps!

There are literally hundreds of different *quilt blocks*. Some were named for, or created in honor of, a special event in the quilters' lives. Examples include *Rocky Road to Kansas, Trail of the Covered Wagons, Wedding Ring,* or *Underground Railroad*. More often, though, it seems they were named after everyday objects and sights: *Log Cabin, Broken Dishes, Flying Geese,* and *Maple Leaf.*

Most of the time a quilt was made up of all one block pattern, but sometimes several different blocks were incorporated into one quilt. A *sampler quilt* was one in which each block was different and was set apart from the others by *sashing* or narrow borders between the blocks.

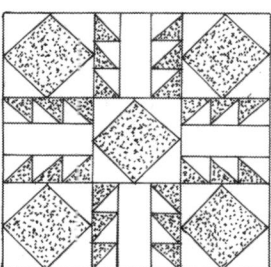

MOTHER'S DREAM

The Quilting Bee

After the lady of the house completed her *quilt top,* her favorite way to finish it was to hold a quilting bee. The quilt would be set up in the hostess's

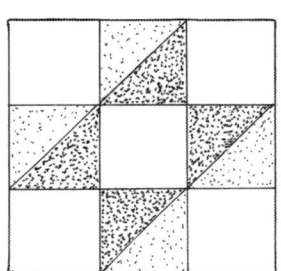

COUNTRY WIFE

home on a quilting frame with all three layers basted together and ready for stitching. Friends and family from the surrounding area would be invited to spend a day quilting and visiting. On the day of the quilting bee, the women and girls arrived early and worked all day on the quilt. While they worked, a huge meal would be cooking on the wood stove. At the end of the day, the men folk came home, and then everyone would eat their fill. After supper, the music would start and the dancing would begin!

Not all quilting bees were such grand affairs—some were small gatherings of a few close friends who came together for a few hours of fellowship and stitching. Whether large or small, the quilting bee gave women a rare opportunity to take a break from their daily routine, relax, and socialize.

CHURN DASH

Quilts were, and still are, functional works of art. They will brighten up a room—and a heart!—today the same way they brightened up the dim, drab prairie cabins of yesterday. Colorful quilts are constant reminders of the beauty and functionality that homemakers bring to those around them.

Saint Zita, Patroness of Homemakers, Pray for Us!

59

Lap Quilt

This little quilt and a good book are all that you need for
a cozy evening by the fire.

To make this 40 by 50-inch lap quilt, you will need the following:

- For the *quilt top,* you will need scraps or small amounts ($1/4$ yard) of different fabrics totaling about $1^1/_2$ yards. These can be solids or prints from your own scrap box, from friends and relatives, from worn-out clothing, or purchased new. You will also need 1 yard of a solid or print fabric that coordinates well with your chosen scraps.

- For the backing, you will need $1^1/_2$ yards of any 60 inch wide fabric. *Muslin* is used many times for *quilt backing.* A sheet also works very well.

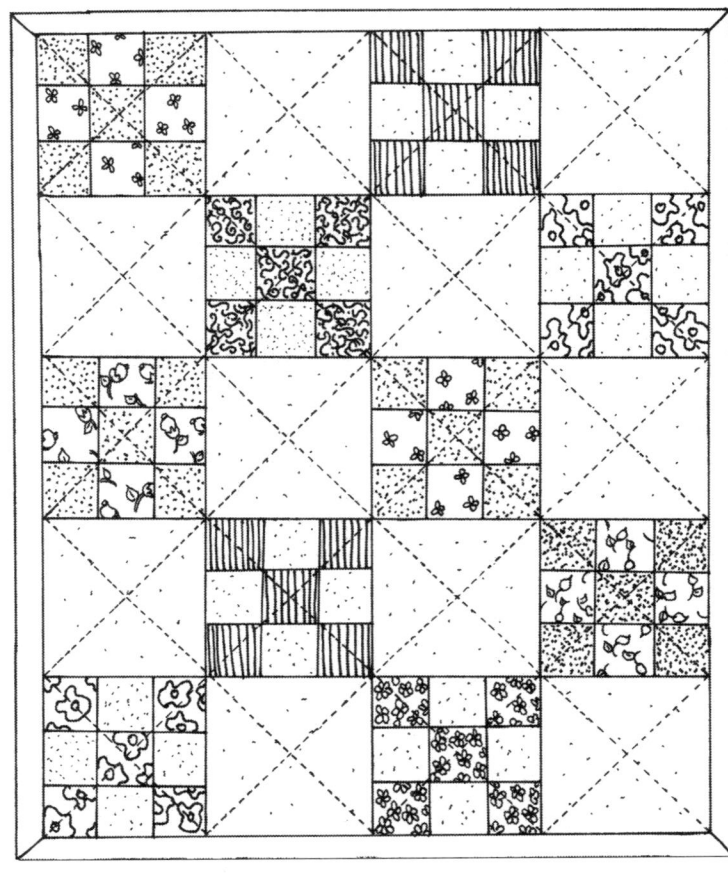

- For *batting,* you can use an old blanket cut down to size or buy new batting. Batting is usually sold by the roll; sometimes it is cut off the bolt by the yard. If you are buying it in a packaged roll, look for "crib size" batting.

- If you plan to stitch your quilt, you will need a quilting hoop (or very large embroidery hoop) and a spool of quilting thread. Or if you are tying it, you will need embroidery floss. See "To Stitch or Tie" on page 64.

- For thread to sew the squares together, choose a neutral color that will blend in with most of your fabric patterns/colors.

Quilts take time, so work on this project a little each day. Don't get discouraged if it seems to be taking longer than you thought it would. The time will be well worth it!

1. The *quilt block* you will be making for your lap quilt will be a *nine-patch*. This is an old pattern that was very popular in the past due to its simplicity (easy to sew) and efficiency (uses up scraps of fabric). The first thing to do is to choose and gather your fabrics. If any are new fabrics, make sure to wash and dry them before you begin cutting.

2. Next, using the "Lap Quilt Block" pattern on page 95, cut 5 squares from a darker fabric and 4 squares from a lighter fabric.

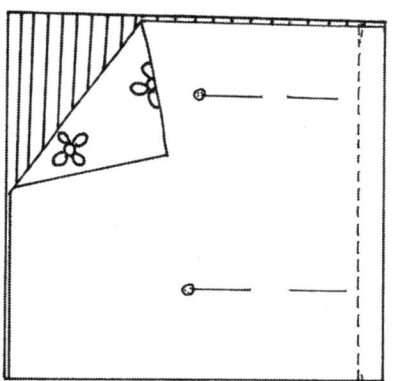

3. Match up and pin 3 pairs of 1 light and 1 dark. Sew these pairs, right sides together, along one side using a $1/4$-inch seam allowance. Now, you should have 3 pairs of squares, each one with a light and a dark square; you will also have 3 leftover single squares: 2 darks and 1 light.

4. Press each pair well, making sure the seams are pressed *open*. Now pin each of the single squares to the end of each of the pairs. When doing this, make sure you are alternating light and dark fabrics. Press open all seams.

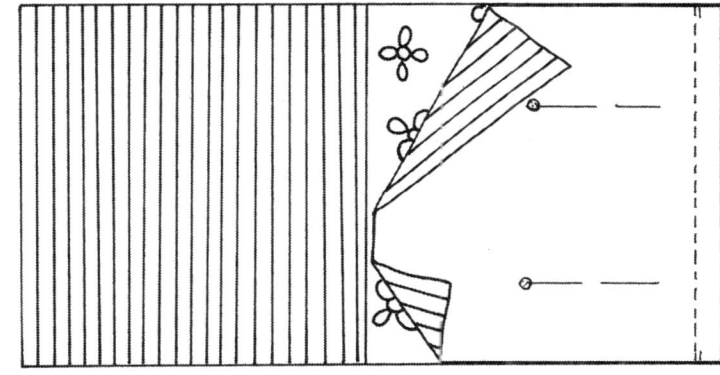

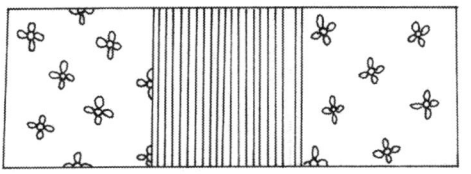

5. Here is an example of what you should now have: 3 rows with 3 squares each, in alternating fabrics. Lay them out on a table top as illustrated.

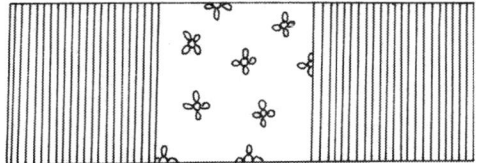

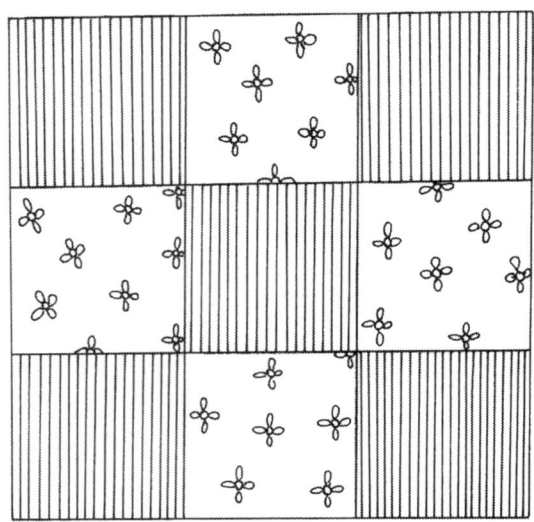

6. Matching all seams be sure right sides are together. Then pin the top row to the middle row and stitch. Press the new seam open. Now pin the bottom row to the middle row, carefully matching the seams, and stitch. Press open this seam also. Your finished, pressed block should measure $10^1/_2$ inches across. Congratulations! You have just completed your first nine-patch quilt block!

7. Continue designing, cutting out, and sewing nine-patch blocks until you have a total of 10. Don't try to do them all at once. If you complete one block a day or even one block a week, soon you will be the proud owner of a new quilt!

"*She makes her own coverlets;*
fine linen and purple are her clothing."
Proverbs 31:22

8. After you have all 10 blocks finished, you will need to make a $10^1/_2$ by $10^1/_2$-inch square pattern on paper. (Any paper will do.) Use a ruler to be sure your pattern is a perfect square that measures $10^1/_2$ inches on all sides. This will be your *template,* or pattern, for the nonpieced blocks that will go between the pieced nine-patch blocks. Cut out 10 of these $10^1/_2$-inch squares.

9. Now you are ready to design the layout of your quilt. The best way to do this is to place the nine-patch blocks and the solid (meaning a single piece of fabric, not necessarily solid in print) blocks on the floor, alternating pieced and solid blocks, in the way in which you think they look best. (*Make sure your quilt is 4 blocks wide and 5 blocks long.*) Doing this gives you an idea of how the finished quilt will look while allowing you the freedom to rearrange it until it is just right.

10. Once you have all the blocks laid out just as you want them, you are ready to sew the squares together. (Please note: You will be sewing squares into rows in very much the same way as you did for the individual blocks.) Begin by picking up the first 2 blocks, a nine-patch and a solid, pin them with right rides together, and sew them with a $^1/_4$-inch seam allowance. Press open this seam and lay the 2 blocks back in their place on the floor.

11. Now, pin the next block to the set of two you have just sewn together; sew it in the same way as the block before. Press open this seam and lay your 3 blocks, which are now stitched together, back in their place on the floor.

12. Repeat step #11 to stitch on the fourth and last block on the top row.

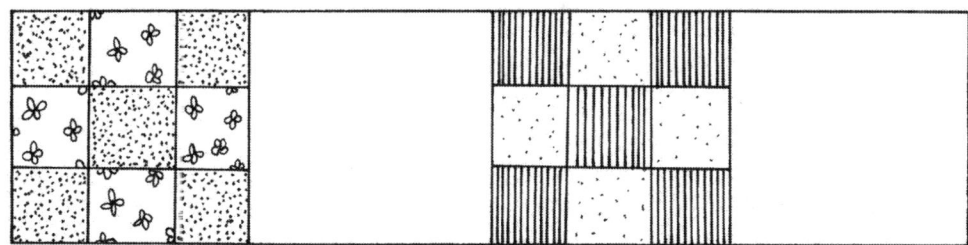

13. Continue sewing blocks together; follow the above steps and use your floor layout as a guide until you have completed all 5 rows. Press open all seams.

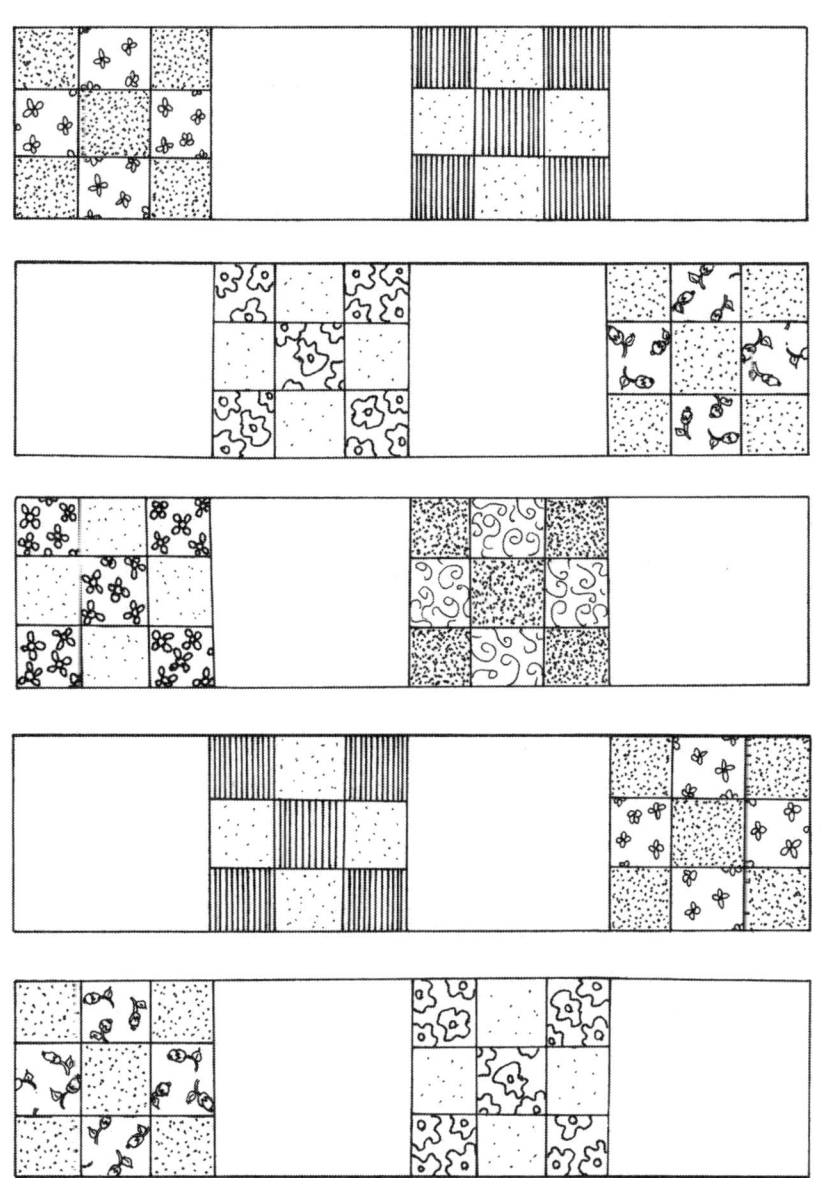

14. Now you are ready to sew the rows together. Start with the first two rows; pin them with right sides together. Match the seams as carefully as you can. Stitch using a $^1/_4$ inch seam allowance and then press open the seam.

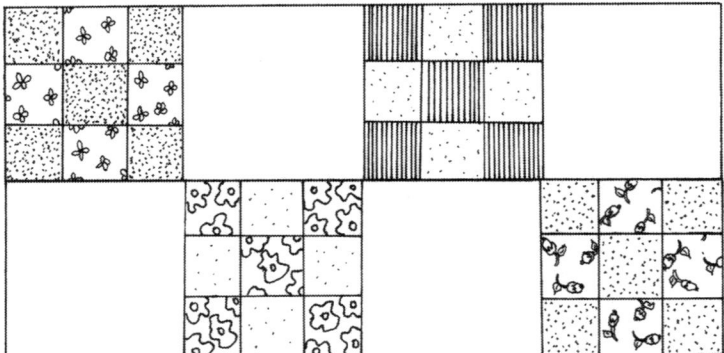

15. Continue sewing the rows together, pressing well after you stitch each seam. When the last row has been sewn on, your *quilt top* is complete!

16. The next step is to put the layers of the quilt together. Make sure the fabric for the *quilt back* has been washed and dried. Lay this fabric wrong side up on the floor. Next, spread the batting out over the backing. Now place the quilt top right side up on top of the batting, being careful to keep everything smooth and wrinkle free. The backing needs to extend at least 3 inches beyond each side of the quilt top. (The backing will probably extend further than 3 inches all around, but the excess can be trimmed away later.)

17. The layers of the quilt must now be basted together with very large basting stitches. These stitches simply serve to hold the layers together while you finish your quilt—they will be removed later. Run the basting stitches across the entire quilt, making the lines of basting no more than 8 inches apart. You are now ready to quilt or tie your quilt!

To Stitch or Tie

There are two ways to finish your quilt: traditional quilting
(or stitching) and tying.

For the first method, you need a very large embroidery hoop, quilting thread, and needles. To begin quilting, position the hoop in the center of the quilt. You can stitch in *any* design you like, but it may be easiest to start with something simple like quilting an "X" in each block using a running stitch. The purpose of these stitches is simply to hold the three layers together and to keep the batting from shifting.

To *tie* your quilt, you will need embroidery floss and a needle. With this method you simply pull the threaded needle in and out; then tie a good knot or make a bow and "double knot" it. Repeat this process all over the quilt; again, be sure the ties are no more than 8 inches apart. Please note: The "in" and "out" of the needle should be very close together, about $^1/_8$ inch.

18. Now that your quilt has been basted together, it can be folded up and put away—take it out when you have a few minutes to work on quilting or tying it. But don't rush—take your time! Most people find this part of the process very relaxing.

19. After the quilt has been fully quilted or tied, you are ready to bind the edges. To do this, you must first trim the *batting* so that it extends only 1 inch beyond the borders of the quilt top. *Be careful not to accidentally cut the quilt back!* Next, trim the quilt back so that it extends out $2^1/_2$ inches from the quilt top or $1^1/_2$ inches from the batting.

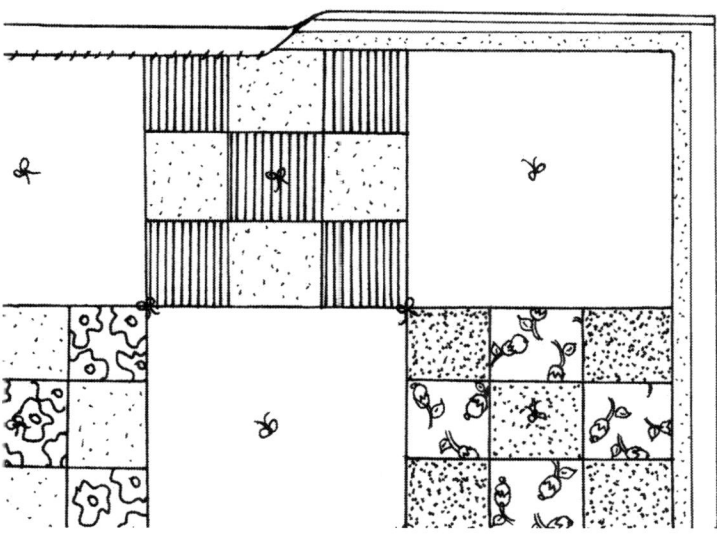

20. To finish the edges, press a $^1/_2$-inch hem in the backing, up toward the quilt top, all around the quilt. Next, fold the quilt back over the batting so that the edge of the back overlaps the quilt top about $^1/_4$ inch. You can either slip stitch or top stitch this in place, but the needle must go through all the layers to hold the *binding* in place.

21. The corners can be mitered, as with the cloth napkins, or simply folded over and stitched down. And that completes your lap quilt! Congratulations!

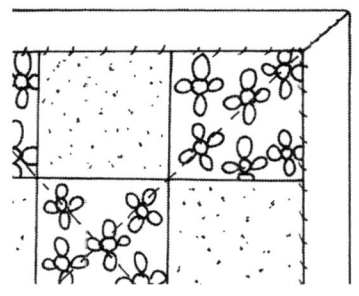

Mitered Corner

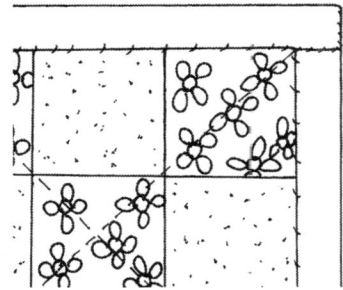

Folded Over and Stitched

❧ The Projects: Gifts ❧

Even though many things in the **Homemaking** section make lovely gifts, the projects here are especially well suited for the occasion of giving.

Each project is labeled with a number to indicate the difficulty level: 1—Beginner; 2—Intermediate.

"Recall the words of the Lord Jesus Himself, Who said, 'There is more happiness in giving than receiving.' "
Acts 20:35

Scented Sachets

These little sachets are wonderful when they are tucked inside your pillowcase. When you lie down, give them a little squeeze to release their scent so you can enjoy their delicate fragrance as you rest. A bundle of three sachets makes a very nice gift!

To make a set of three scented sachets, you will need the following:

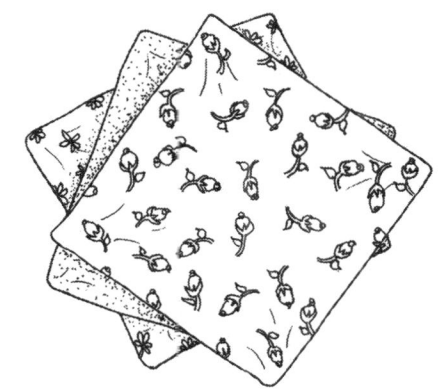

- 6 squares cut from the "Scented Sachet" pattern on page 97. This project is perfect for those scraps of cotton cloth you've been saving. Calicos and other floral prints look very pretty.

- Potpourri or other scented filler. The best filler to use for "sleep sachets" is pure lavender flowers—these smell heavenly and keep their scent for a very long time. Check your local craft or health-food store for lavender flowers.

- Thread to match.

1. Follow steps 1 through 5 in the "Pincushion" project on page 36. The steps are the same except that the opening you will leave in step 3 will be about $1^1/_2$ inches instead of 2 inches.

2. For filling the little sachets, a small spoon works well. Be careful not to overfill! They only need to be about half full.

3. After filling, carefully stitch the opening closed using a slip stitch as shown in the illustration. You can use a double thread if you like, but a single will work just fine.

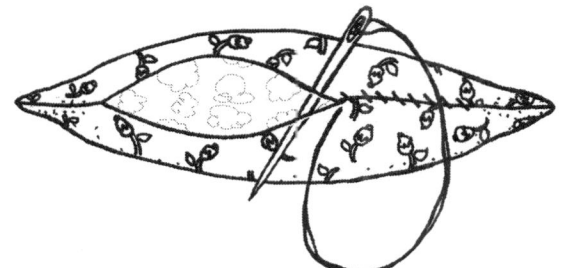

4. These sachets look especially nice when stacked one on top of the other and tied together with a pretty ribbon.

❧❧ Hair Scrunchie ❧❧

This can be made from a scrap from one of your previous projects. Or, if you're giving it as a gift, purchase a bit of fabric in the recipient's favorite color or style.

To make a scrunchie for yourself or a friend, you will need the following:

- A piece of fabric 5 inches wide by 22 inches long. If you are buying new fabric, ask for a piece about 7 inches wide to allow for shrinkage when you wash and dry it.

- A piece of $1/4$ inch wide elastic cut 7 inches long. (A note about elastic: There are many different types; some can be difficult to use. Look for the ones labeled "soft stretch.")

- Thread to match.

1. After washing and drying your fabric, cut a strip 5 inches wide by 22 inches long. Fold the fabric in half lengthwise with the right sides together. Stitch along the *long* side with a $1/4$-inch seam allowance. Do not stitch the ends yet.

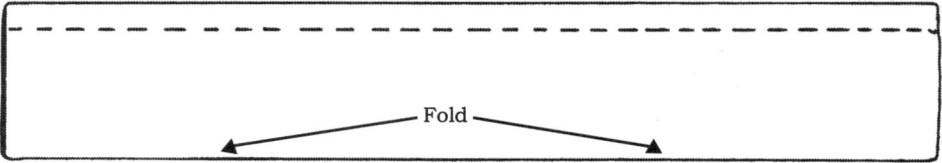

— Fold —

2. Turn the scrunchie so that the right side is out and press flat with the seam on the edge. Carefully tuck in a $1/4$-inch hem on one end and press. Do not stitch the hem closed yet.

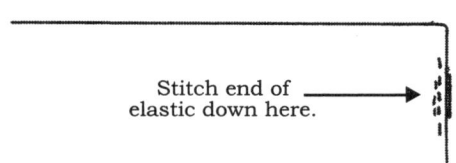

Stitch end of elastic down here.

3. Cut a 7-inch piece of elastic. Fasten a safety pin to one end of the elastic and start running the elastic through the tube from the *unhemmed* end. Do not pull the elastic all the way through, but stop when the end of the elastic is even with the end of the tube. To hold the elastic in place, stitch well, close to the edge of the fabric.

4. After stitching the end of the elastic in place, grip the safety pin inside the fabric and pull the elastic to the other end of the scrunchie. The fabric will "scrunch up" as you go. Pull the elastic a few inches past the end of the fabric. Lay $1/4$ inch of the elastic across the fabric on the other end of the scrunchie. Stitch down well to hold in place.

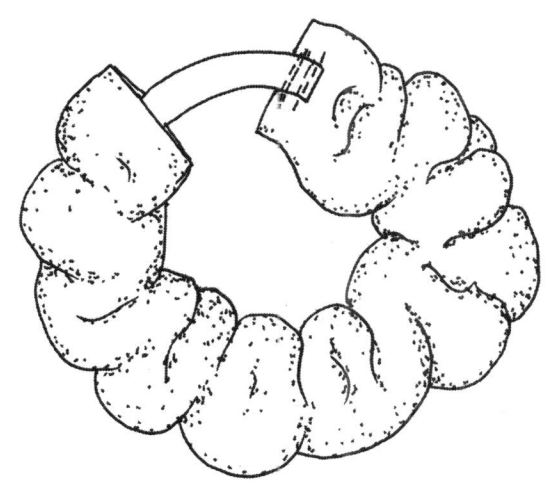

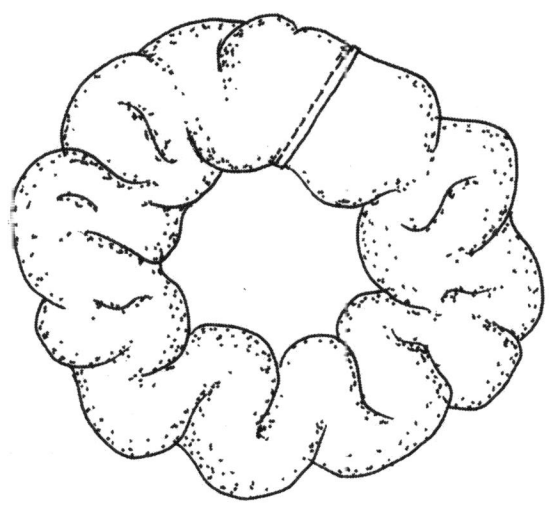

5. Now, pull the end with the $1/4$-inch hem over the other end of the scrunchie, overlapping it $1/2$ inch. Pin to hold in place; then stitch through all layers $1/8$ inch from the hemmed edge.

6. You can now add any embellishments you might want, such as tiny ribbon roses or little stitched-on beads. Or you can leave it plain, simple, and beautiful!

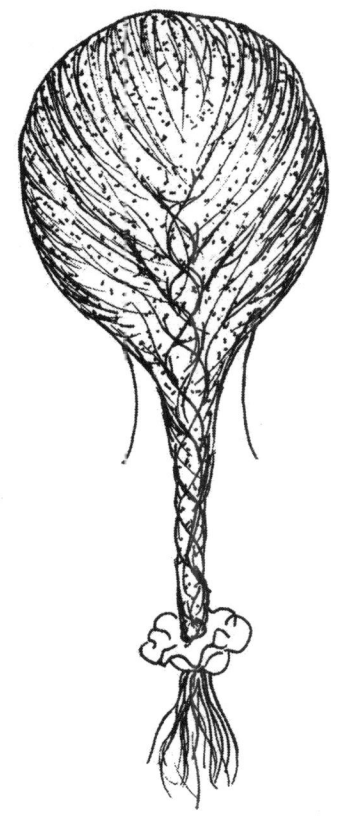

Mary's Mantle

This beautiful little mantle can be draped gracefully over the shoulders of most small statues of the Blessed Mother. It makes a lovely gift for a friend in honor of one of Our Lady's special feast days.

To make a special mantle for Mary, you will need the following:

- $1/4$ yard of fabric. Avoid heavy-weight fabrics. You can also use any scraps you may have on hand.

- $1/8$ inch wide satin ribbon. This is sold by the spool for less than a dollar. For one mantle you will need about 12 inches of ribbon.

- Thread to match.

- Any creative embellishments you wish: trims and lace, ribbon roses, beads, "gem stones," glitter, or even paint!

1. The patterns on page 99 are sized for 6- to 8-inch statues. If yours is bigger, simply enlarge the largest pattern on all sides $1/2$ inch for every inch of statue. Your 6-inch statue will measure about $4^1/_2$ inches from shoulders to feet and an 8-inch statue will be about $5^1/_2$ or 6 inches from shoulder to feet. (Your statue must have its "neck" free to be able to wear the mantle.) Once you have the correct pattern size for your statue, use it to cut one mantle from your piece of fabric.

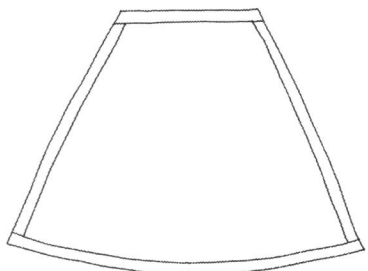

2. First, press to the wrong side a $1/4$-inch hem on the two *sides* of the mantle. Next, press a $1/4$-inch hem on the top and bottom.

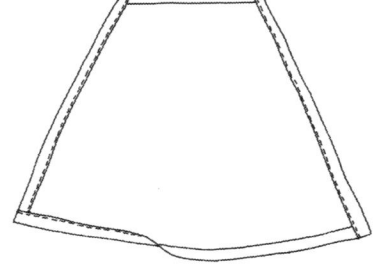

3. Now, turn the sides again another $1/4$ inch and stitch down. Do this to the bottom hem as well. Press well.

72

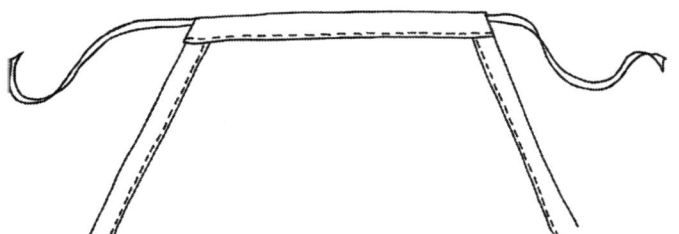

4. At the top of the mantle, turn another $1/4$ inch and press. Lift the hem slightly and lay the $1/8$ inch wide ribbon in the crease. Stitch down close to the edge of the hem being careful not to catch the ribbon in your stitches.

5. Give the mantle a final press. You are now ready to decorate it in a way that befits the Queen of Heaven and Earth! Use your imagination and whatever materials you have on hand. Since this will not need to be laundered as clothing would, you can use almost anything for embellishment. You could even "draw" one of Mary's monograms or a crown using glue and then cover the glue with glitter. To attach the mantle to your statue of Mary, just take the ribbon ends and tie a bow around Mary's neck. You can even make different mantles for Mary's different feast days!

Here is a list of feast days on which Mary can wear her new mantle. You might want to decorate and include this list with the mantle if you are giving it as a gift.

~ Solemnity of Mary (January 1)	~ Assumption (August 15)
~ Presentation of Our Lord (February 2)	~ Queenship of Mary (August 22)
~ Our Lady of Lourdes (February 11)	~ Birth of Mary (September 8)
~ Annunciation (March 25)	~ Our Lady of Sorrows (September 15)
~ The month of May is Mary's month!	~ Our Lady of the Rosary (October 7)
~ Visitation (May 31)	~ Presentation of Mary (November 21)
~ Immaculate Heart (3rd Saturday after Pentecost)	~ Immaculate Conception (December 8)
~ Our Lady of Mt. Carmel (July 16)	~ Our Lady of Guadalupe (December 12)

Jar Lid Cover

This will dress up a gift of homemade jelly or
jam—or simply make the pantry shelves pretty!

To make a jar lid cover, you will need the following:

- Scrap of fabric at least 8 by 8 inches. If you are buying new fabric, ask for $^1/_4$ yard. "Homespun" plaids and old-fashioned little calicos will look pretty.

- 9 inches of $^1/_4$-inch-wide elastic. If you made a hair scrunchie, the leftover elastic will work well. If you are buying new elastic, look for "soft stretch" on the label.

- Thread to match.

1. First, cut out one circle using the "Jar Lid Cover" pattern on page 101. Using a pencil, lightly mark the elastic placement line.

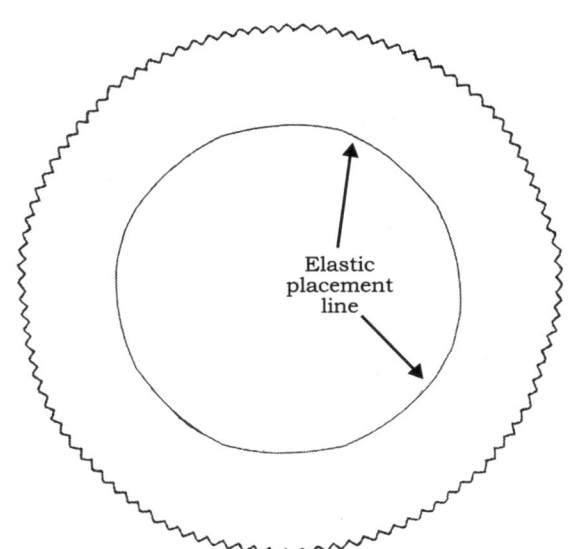

Elastic
placement
line

2. Turn under $^1/_4$ inch all the way around and press. Then turn under another $^1/_4$-inch, press, and stitch. If you want to simply "pink" the edges with pinking shears, cut the fabric with the pinking shears along the line indicated on the pattern. To keep the "pinked" edges from fraying, you can also apply a product called "Fray Check." You can buy this wherever sewing notions are sold. Follow the directions on the label.

3. Cut a 9-inch-long piece of elastic. Form a circle; be sure it overlaps 1 inch at the ends. Stitch the ends together.

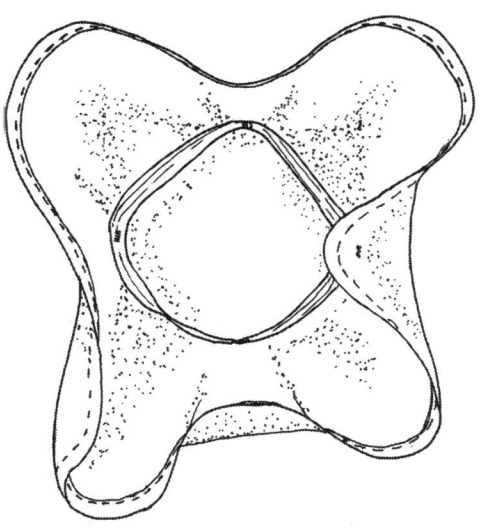

4. Fold the fabric in quarters and press to mark the fold lines. Then fold the elastic in quarters and mark the fold lines with a pencil. Using a needle and thread, attach the elastic to the fabric at the fold lines along the placement line.

5. Stretching the elastic as you go, machine or hand stitch the elastic along the placement line between the points where you have attached it.

6. If your jar lid cover is a gift for someone, add a finishing touch: tie a ribbon or a bit of raffia around the top, over the elastic area.

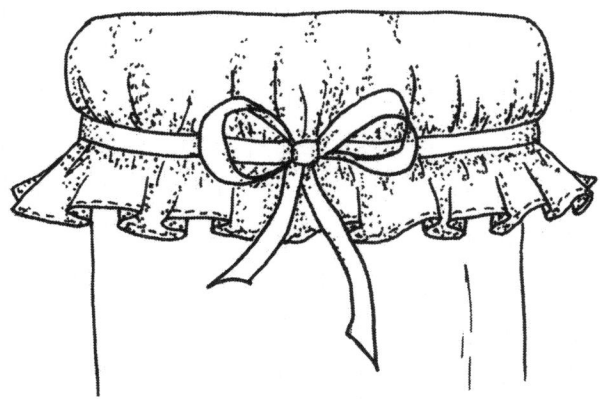

More Ideas

If you store your buttons in jars, these covers will add a nice touch. Also, in addition to putting them on jars of jams and jellies, try this gift idea:

Fill a quart jar with the dry ingredients for your favorite homemade pancake, muffin, or cookie recipe. Screw on the lid and add a pretty lid cover. On an index or recipe card, write out the directions and the "wet" ingredients (such as eggs, milk, etc.) needed; then attach the card to the jar with a piece of ribbon or raffia. A quick and delicious gift!

Baby Blanket

This warm, cuddly blanket is bigger than a typical receiving blanket. It makes a great gift for a new brother, sister, or cousin.

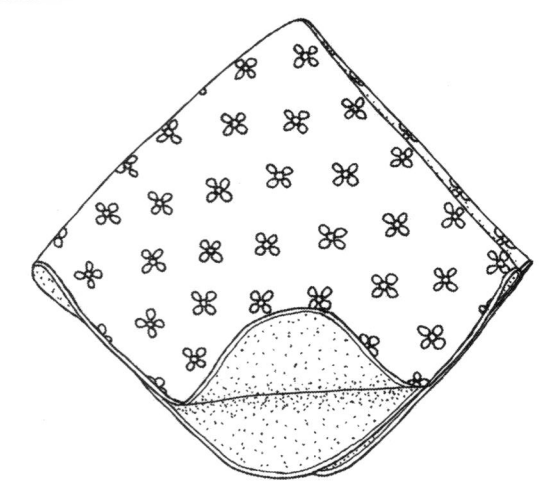

To make this baby blanket, you will need the following:

- $1^3/_8$ yards of a nice cotton flannel.

- A package of double-fold bias tape in a color that coordinates with your chosen fabric. Make sure the package contains at least 5 yards of bias tape. If it does not, you will need 2 packages.

- Thread to match the bias tape.

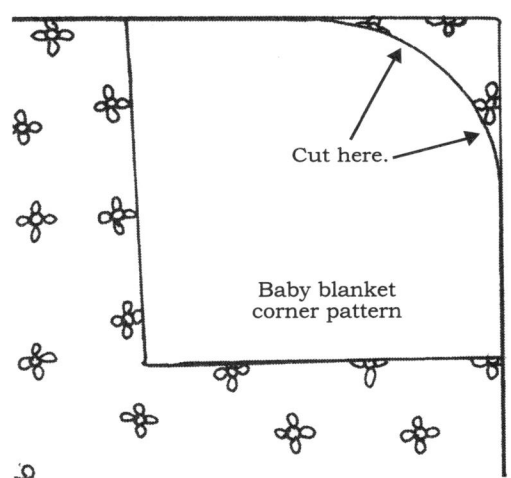

Cut here.

Baby blanket corner pattern

1. After you wash and dry the flannel, make sure it is on grain (See "Choosing and Preparing Fabric" on page 33.). The next step is to round off the corners. To do this, place the "Baby Blanket Corner" pattern (see page 103) on the fabric and cut away the corner. Make sure you are careful to line up the edges of the pattern with the edges of the fabric. Trim any loose threads and make the edges neat and clean.

2. Unfold the double-fold bias tape and pin it to the blanket with right sides together and raw edges even. When you reach the point where you began, overlap the end of the tape $1^1/_4$ inch. Be careful not to stretch the bias tape as you pin it. Stitch along the first $1/_4$-inch crease.

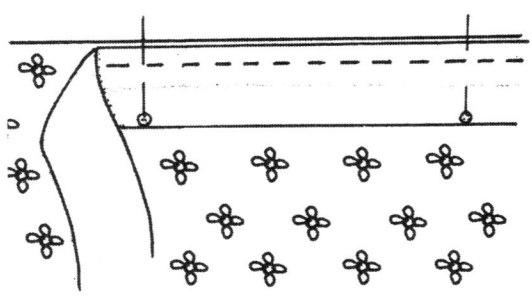

3. Next, fold the bias tape over to enclose the seam allowance; then stitch down. Turn under $^1/_4$ inch at the very end for a neat finish.

4. If you need to join two pieces of bias tape together to get a strip long enough, the best way to do it is by sewing the pieces at an angle. (You will notice that this is how the manufacturer does it.) To do this, simply match up the ends at a right angle with the right sides together. You will need to unfold the ends to do this. Let the ends overlap each other slightly and pin in place. Stitch as shown, from one outside corner to the next. Trim away the excess, leaving $^1/_4$ inch. Straighten and press to replace the creases.

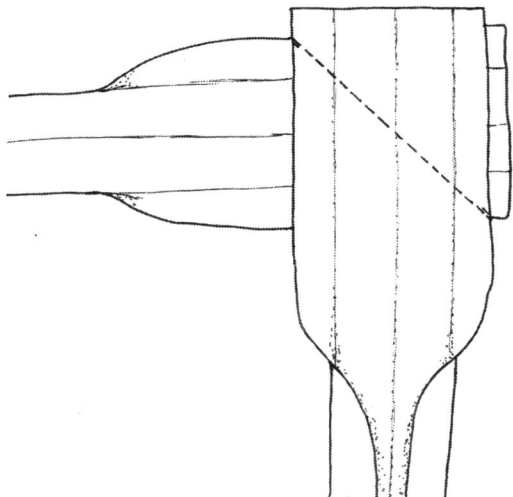

A nice finishing touch would be to embroider the baby's name and date of birth (or baptismal date) in one of the corners of the blanket.

 # Baby Bib

The flannel lining in this little bib makes it very absorbent. It would make a great first birthday gift!

To make the baby bib, you will need the following:

- $3/8$ yard of fabric of your choice. Some ideas for the outer fabric might be florals or pastels for girls and plaids or stripes for boys. The front and the back of the bib do not have to be of the same fabric. There could be a print on one side and a solid on the other! Always try to use what you have on hand before buying any new fabric.

- $3/8$ yard white or off-white flannel for the lining.

- A pack of double-fold bias tape.

- A package of assorted snaps. For this project you will use one of the large ones, but buying an assorted pack allows you more choices for future projects.

- Thread to match bias tape.

- Optional: button or ribbon-rose.

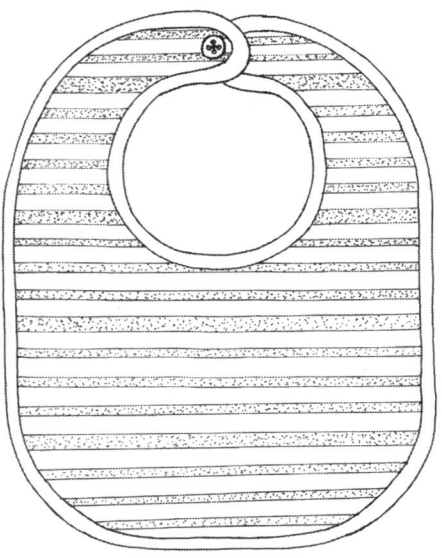

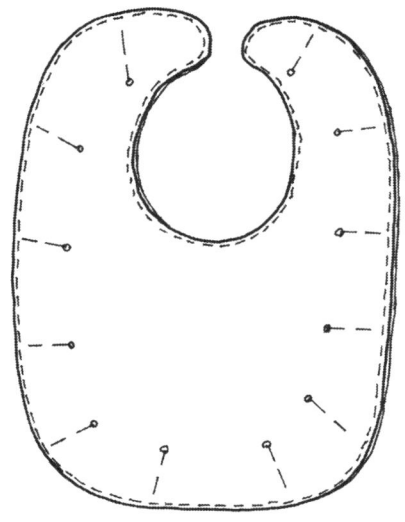

1. After washing and drying your fabric, use the "Baby Bib" pattern on pages 105 and 107 to cut out 2 bib pieces from the outer fabric and 1 from the flannel.

2. Next, make a sandwich with the flannel in the middle and the "pretty" fabric on the top and bottom, right sides *out*. Pin in place and then stitch around the whole bib very close to the edge (less than $1/4$ inch, if possible).

2. Unfold the double-fold bias tape and pin it along the edges of the baby bib with right sides together and raw edges even. Be careful not to stretch the bias tape as you pin it. When you reach the point where you began, overlap the end of the tape $1^1/_4$ inch. Stitch along the first $^1/_4$-inch crease.

3. Next, fold the bias tape over to enclose the seam allowance; then stitch down. Turn under $^1/_4$ inch at the very end for a neat finish. It is a good idea to begin sewing the bias tape at the top of the bib (which will be behind the baby's head) so that this will be where you finish sewing the tape. That way, the spot where the ends join will be hidden when the bib is being worn.

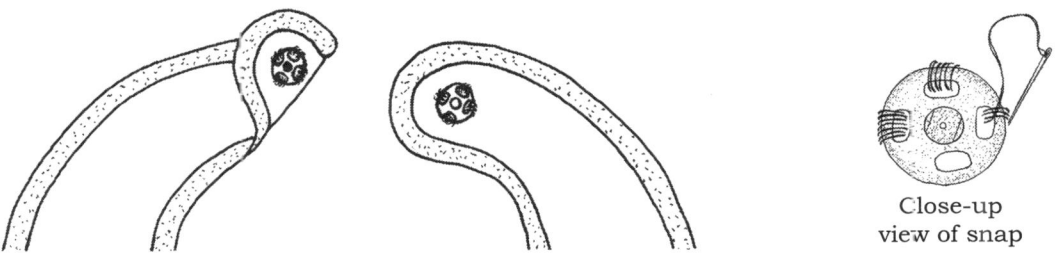

Close-up
view of snap

4. Now, select a snap from among the largest on your card of assorted snaps. Make sure you have marked with a pencil the spots where the two halves of the snap will go. Take one half of a snap and position it over your mark. Use a double-threaded needle to sew a couple of anchoring stitches to hold it in place. Continue stitching the snap in place, using all four of its holes.

5. Add a button or a little ribbon-rose to the outside of the top snap for a nice finishing touch. This will also help cover the stitches that came through when you sewed on the snap.

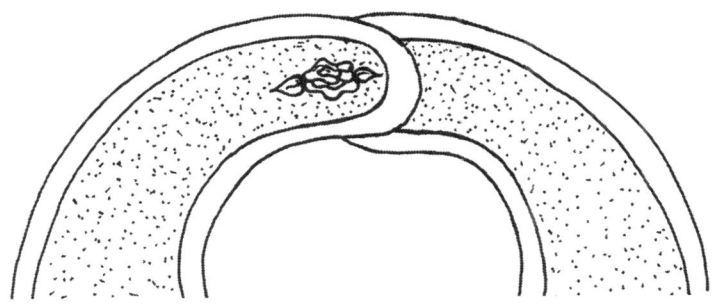

Fabric Gift Bag

This little bag is perfect for a small gift such as a rosary, a medal of a saint, a holy card, or one of the smaller projects in this book! This bag can really be made in any size you want. If you need a larger bag, just begin with a bigger piece of fabric and a longer drawstring.

To make a fabric gift bag, you will need the following:

- A piece of fabric that is slightly taller than it is wide. You can use the "Gift Bag" pattern on page 109 or make it the size you need.

- $1/4$- to $1/2$-inch wide ribbon. If you are using the pattern provided, you will need 16 inches. If you are making your own pattern, the drawstring will need to extend at least 3 inches beyond the edge of each side.

- Thread to match.

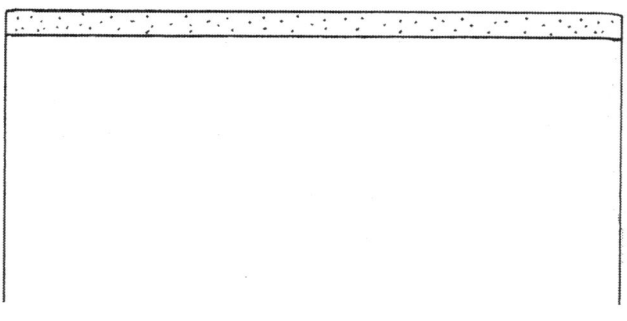

1. The first step is to press a $1/4$-inch hem toward the wrong side, along the top of the bag. The top will be one of the short sides of your rectangle.

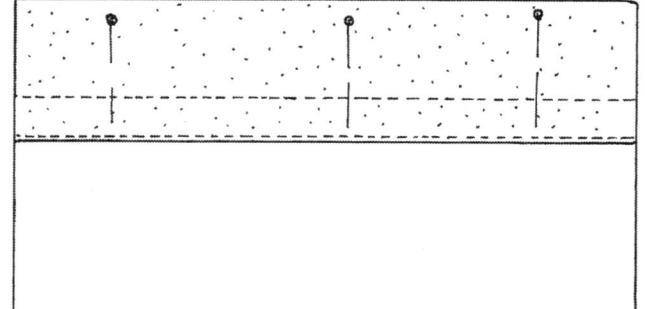

2. Next, turn the same edge down $1^1/4$ inch and press well. Pin in place.

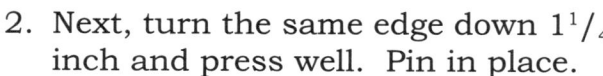

3. Stitch very close to the edge of the hem along the whole length. Now make a second row of stitching $3/8$ inch from the first. A good way to gauge this distance is position your fabric so that the first line of stitching runs right along side (close, but not touching) the *presser foot* as you stitch the second. This distance is usually about $3/8$ inch. Don't worry—perfection is not necessary. ☺

4. Now you have a *casing*. Using a small safety pin as a *bodkin*, pin it to the end of the ribbon. If you are using ribbon wider than $1/4$ inch, you will need to fold the end of the ribbon in half (lengthwise) and then pin it. Run the safety pin through the casing.

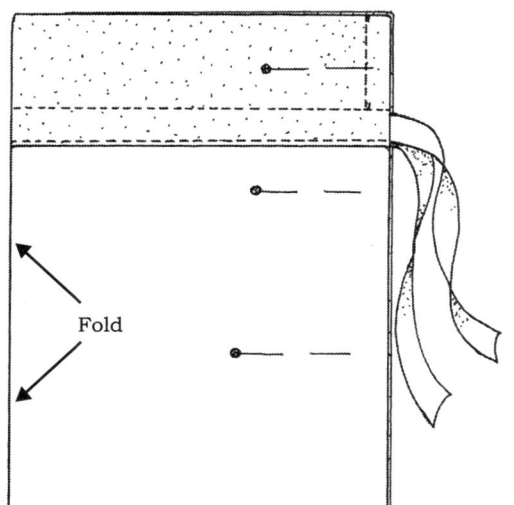

Fold

5. Fold the bag in half and pin. Make sure the ribbons are well out of the way; then stitch with a $1/4$-inch seam allowance from the top of the bag down to the upper row of stitching for the casing. *Do not go past this stitching.* Doing so will catch the drawstring in such a way that it will not work properly.

6. Next, pull the ribbons inside and up. They should be coming out of the top of the bag. Adjust the top pin to hold them in place and out of the way. Beginning at the lower stitching, continue sewing down the side of the bag and then across the bottom.

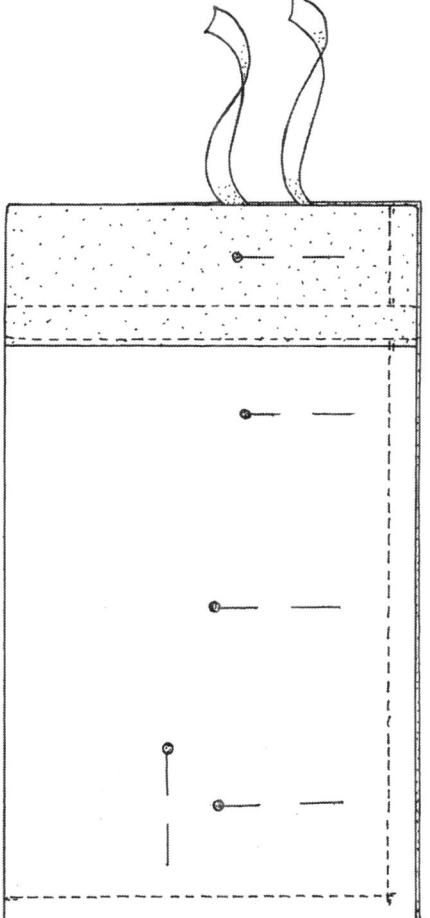

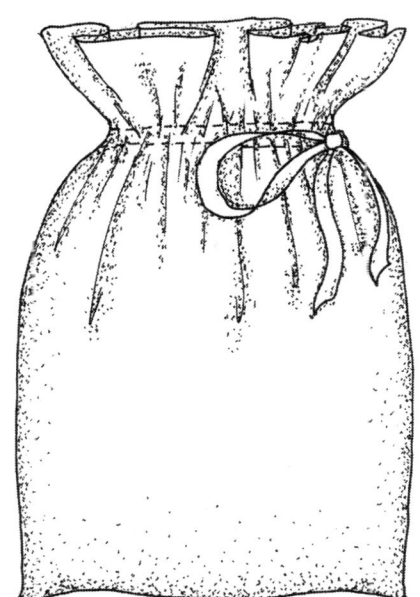

7. Now turn the little gift bag over and press. You are done!

Glossary

Backstitch	A backstitch is used to anchor a thread when beginning or ending a line of stitching. It is also used in hand sewing in areas where a strong seam is needed. See page 17.
Basting	Larger and slightly loose stitches used to temporarily hold fabric in place. See page 16.
Batting	The sheet of filling that goes between the top and bottom of a quilt or pot holder. See pages 48 and 60.
Bias Trim or Tape	A length of cloth cut on the bias, or diagonal, of the fabric. Cutting on the diagonal allows the tape to stretch slightly, which makes going around curves easier to do. See page 48.
Blend	A blend is a fabric with more than one type of fiber woven into it.
Blind Stitching	A type of stitching used when it is not desirable to have the threads show. See page 20.
Bobbin	The smaller spool of thread situated beneath the needle on a sewing machine. See page 29.
Bobbin Thread	The thread located under the needle on a sewing machine. See page 29.
Bodkin	A large needle or tool, sometimes flat, with a large eye for threading ribbon or cord through casings and hems. See page 18.
Casing	A long, narrow fabric tube that is left open on both ends to allow a drawstring, ribbon, or cord to be passed through. See page 81.
Chatelaine	A decorative ornament with several chains falling from it; various sewing and personal articles hang from the chains. See page 18.
Cross Stitch	A simple embroidery stitch that resembles a series of 'X's. See page 27.
Embroider	The art of embellishing cloth with various types of needlework. See page 27.

Embroidery Floss	Special thread for embroider work that is made up of six individual stands. Any number of threads, from one to six, can be used at once. See page 27.
Embroidery Hoop	The wooden or plastic hoop used to hold the fabric tight while embroidery work is being done. See page 10.
Eyelet	A type of cloth or trim with many small holes arranged in a decorative pattern. See page 42.
Gather	To collect fabric along a row of stitching to add fullness or a ruffle. See page 24.
Grain	The threads running the length and the width of the fabric. See page 33.
Hem	The turned and stitched edge of an item or piece of fabric. See page 20.
Homespun	A type of cloth that resembles the old fabrics woven on looms at home. The cloth is usually cotton and has a plaid or check design.
Miter	A corner formed by fitting together two ends of fabric at an angle. See page 44.
Natural Fiber	Any cloth or thread that is from natural sources. See page 35.
Needle Case	A small, round tube, having a bottom and a removable top, used for carrying and storing needles. See page 14.
Nine-Patch	A type of pieced quilt block consisting of three rows of three squares each. The squares can be made up of triangles, rectangles, or even smaller squares, thereby making this one of the most versatile quilt block patterns. See page 61.
Overcast Finish	A type of seam finish used to whip stitch together both seam allowances. See page 19.
Pincushion Box	A small hinged box containing a small pincushion, traditionally hung from a chatelaine. See page 14.
Pinking Shears	Scissors with notched blade edges; it is sometimes used to trim fabrics with an evenly notched edge that resists raveling. See page 40.
Presser Foot	The part on a sewing machine that holds the fabric in place while the needle stitches. See page 80.
Quilt Backing	The piece of cloth that makes up the back layer of a quilt. See page 64.

Quilt Block	A pieced-together or solid component of the quilt top. Quilt blocks can be almost any size or shape and are sewn together to form the top layer of a quilt. See page 58.
Quilt Top	The pieced, decorative top layer of a quilt. See page 59.
Quilting	The act of sewing together the top, center, and back layers of a quilt using many small stitches. See page 58.
Raw Edge	The edge of a piece of fabric that has been cut or torn; a non-finished edge of a piece of fabric.
Right Side	The printed side of a piece of fabric; the side intended to show in the finished product.
Satin Stitch	An embroidery stitch used to fill in areas in the embroidered design. The threads in this stitch lie parallel to each other and very close together, thus creating a smooth "satin" appearance. See page 27.
Seam Allowance	The space between the stitching and the edge of the fabric. The recommended seam allowance for a pattern can be anywhere from $5/8$ inch to $1/4$ inch. Most mass produced patterns use $5/8$-inch seam allowance, but many of the smaller pattern companies use a $1/2$-inch allowance. See page 12.
Seam Finish	The stitching of the seam allowance to prevent unraveling or fraying. See page 19.
Selvage	The tightly woven edges of a piece of cloth that run the length of the fabric. See page 33.
Slip Stitch	A stitch used to close an opening. See page 37.
Top Stitching	A basic running stitch, used in a hem or other location, sewn with the intention of its being visible in the finished product. See page 21.
Warp	The threads running lengthwise in a piece of cloth. They are parallel to the selvage. See page 33.
Weft	The threads across the warp in a piece of cloth. They run perpendicular to the selvage. These threads can also be called the "woof." See page 33.
Whip Stitching	An overcast stitch usually sewn on the edge of the fabric. See page 19.
Wrong Side	The side of the fabric which is not printed on; the side not intended to be visible in the finished product.

Further Reading

My Little House Sewing Book by Margaret Irwin. Published by Harper Festival, 1997.

The Quilt Block History of Pioneer Days by Mary Cobb. Published by The Millbrook press, 1995. (This is not a sewing book, but it contains great information on several quilt blocks and many nonsewing projects for kids.)

Cotton Now & Then~ Fabric Making from Boll to Bolt by Karen Bates Willing & Julie Bates Dock. Published by Now & Then Publications, 1996. (This is a great little book showing all the steps involved in the production of cotton.)

Quilting Now & Then by Karen Bates Willing & Julie Bates Dock. Published by Now & Then Publications, 1994.

Saints, Signs, & Symbols by W. Ellwood Post. Published by Morehouse Publishing, 2001.

Make Your Own Old-Fashioned Cloth Doll and Her Wardrobe by Claire Bryant. Published by Dover Publications, 1990. (This book comes with all the full-sized patterns required to make the sweet doll and all her beautiful clothes.)

Two-Hour Dolls' Clothes by Anita Louise Crane. Published by Sterling Publishing Co., Inc, 1999. (This is a fun book filled with patterns and ideas for clothes for dolls 12 to 18 inches *and* small teddy bears!)

Patterns

The patterns on the following pages can either be copied on a photocopier or traced using tracing paper. After copying or tracing the pattern, cut it out with paper scissors, *not* your fabric scissors. Using your fabric shears for paper will quickly dull them!

To use a pattern you have cut out, pin it to the fabric with the arrows *parallel* to the selvage or *with* the grain. Or you can use a pencil to trace the pattern onto the fabric, but the arrows on the pattern must always line up with the grain of the fabric.

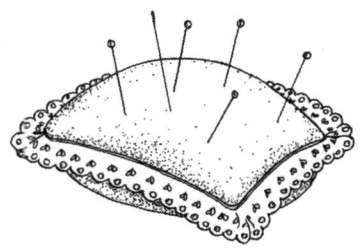

PINCUSHION PATTERN

See page 36 for project instructions.

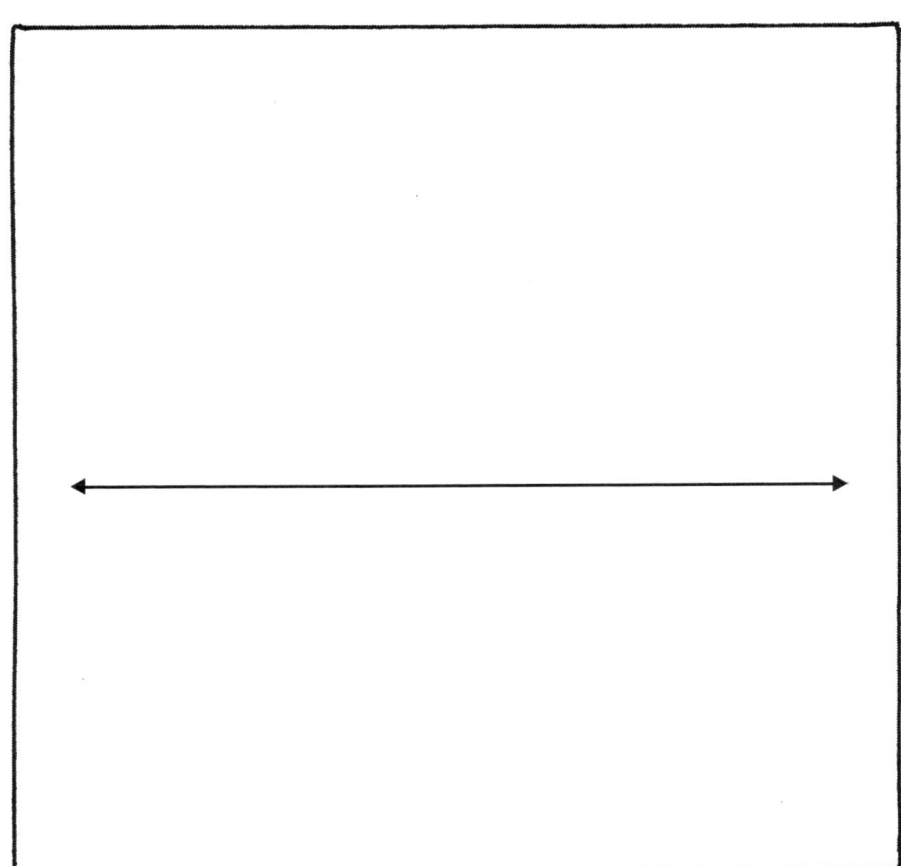

POT HOLDER PATTERN

See page 48 for project instructions.

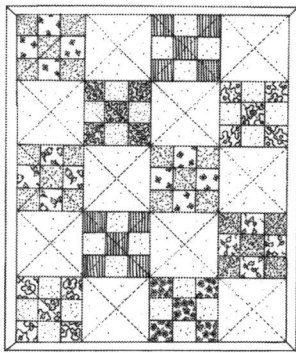

LAP QUILT BLOCK PATTERN

See page 61 for project instructions.

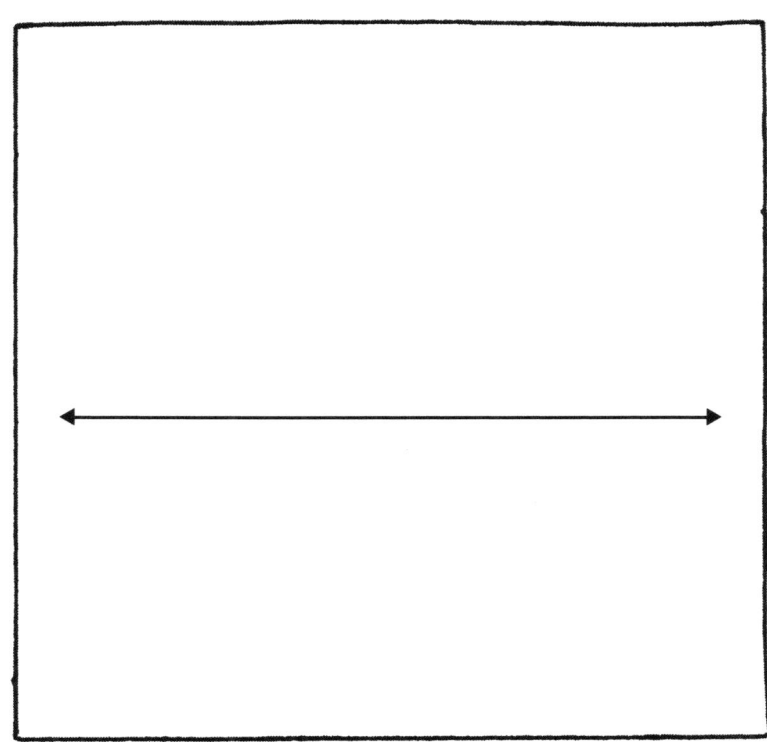

SCENTED SACHET PATTERN

See page 69 for project instructions.

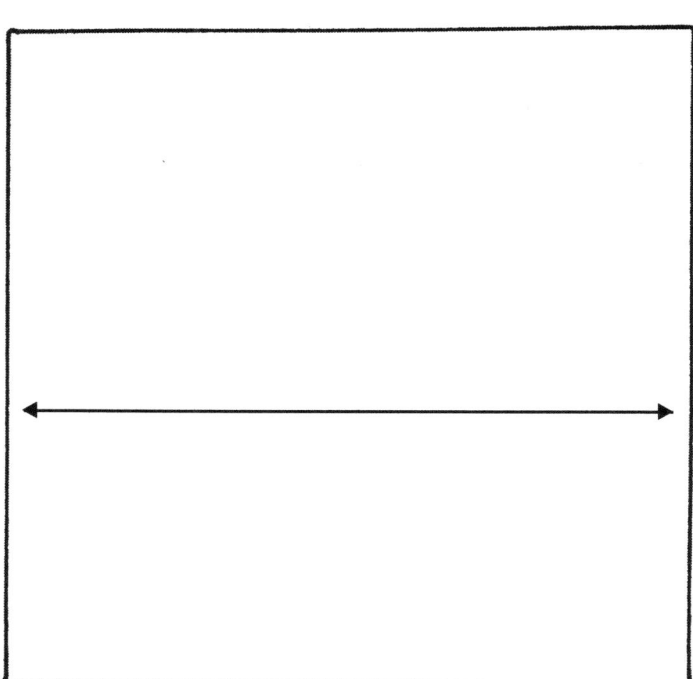

MARY'S MANTLE PATTERN

See page 72 for project instructions.

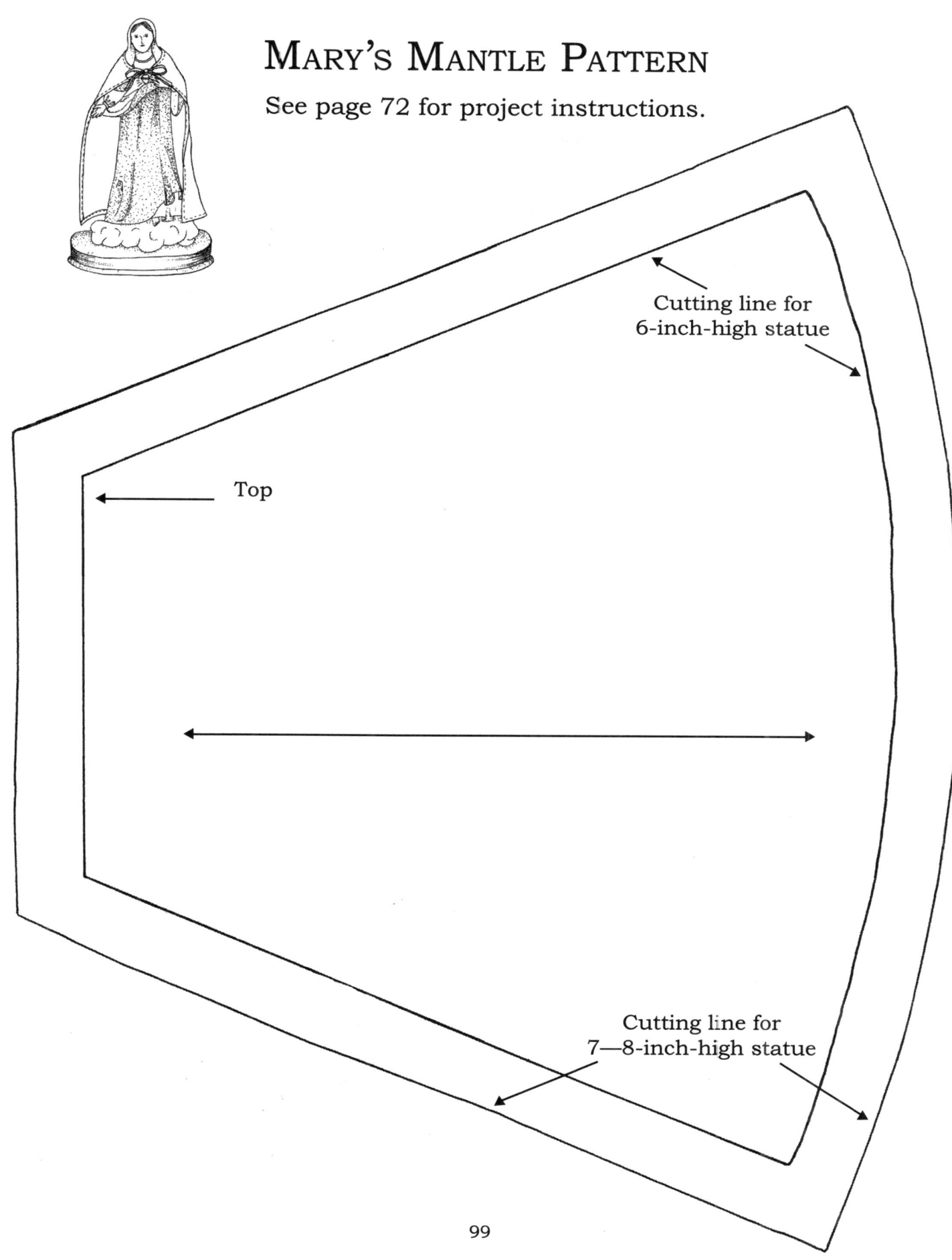

Cutting line for
6-inch-high statue

Top

Cutting line for
7—8-inch-high statue

JAR LID COVER PATTERN

Cut one on fold. See page 74 for project instructions.

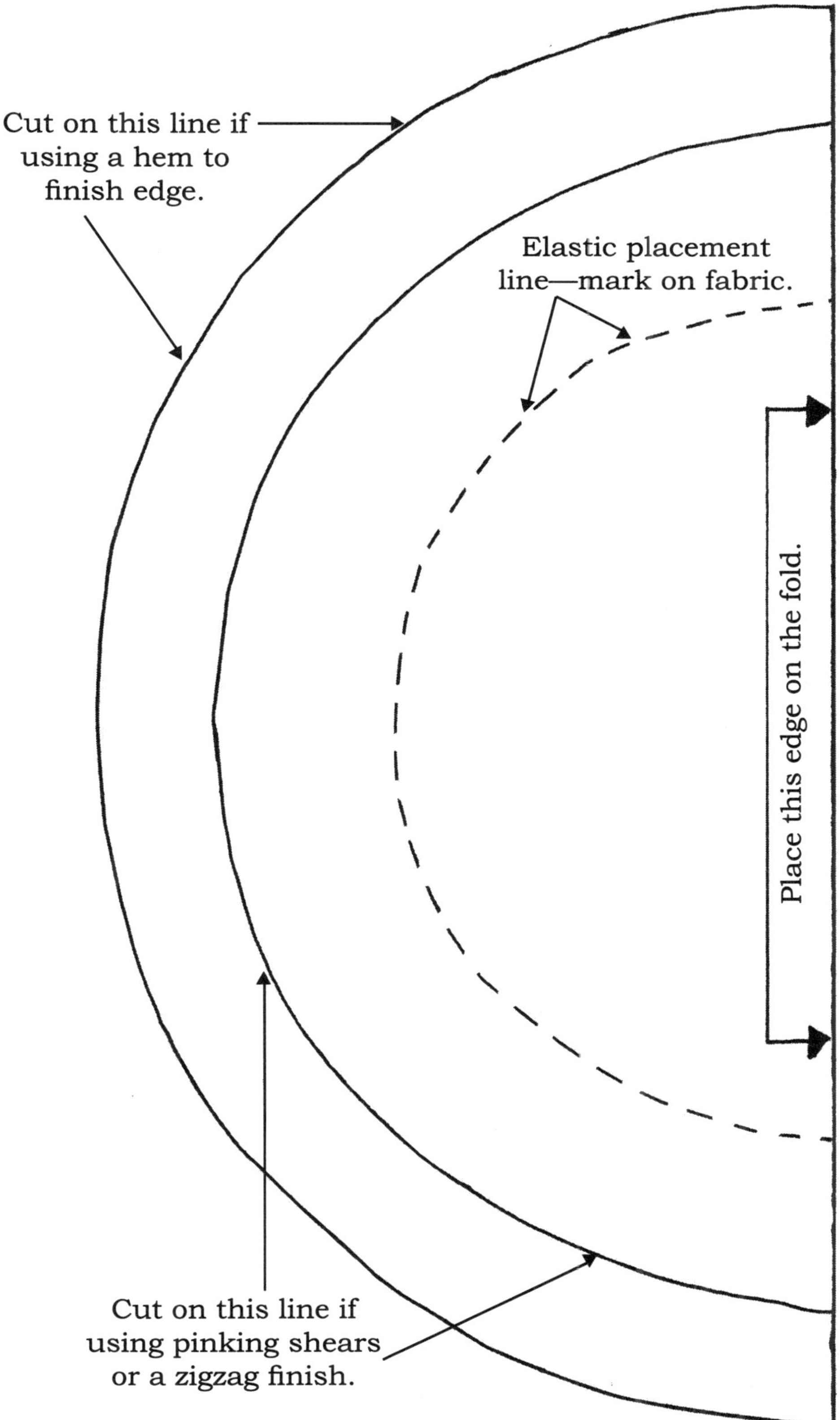

Cut on this line if
using a hem to
finish edge.

Elastic placement
line—mark on fabric.

Place this edge on the fold.

Cut on this line if
using pinking shears
or a zigzag finish.

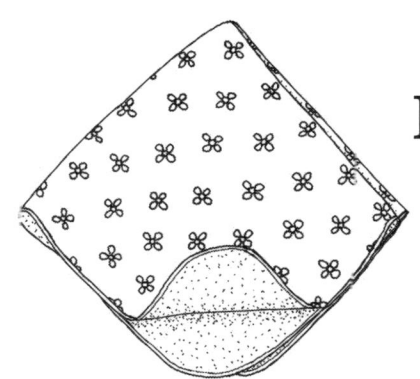

BABY BLANKET CORNER PATTERN

See page 76 for project instructions.

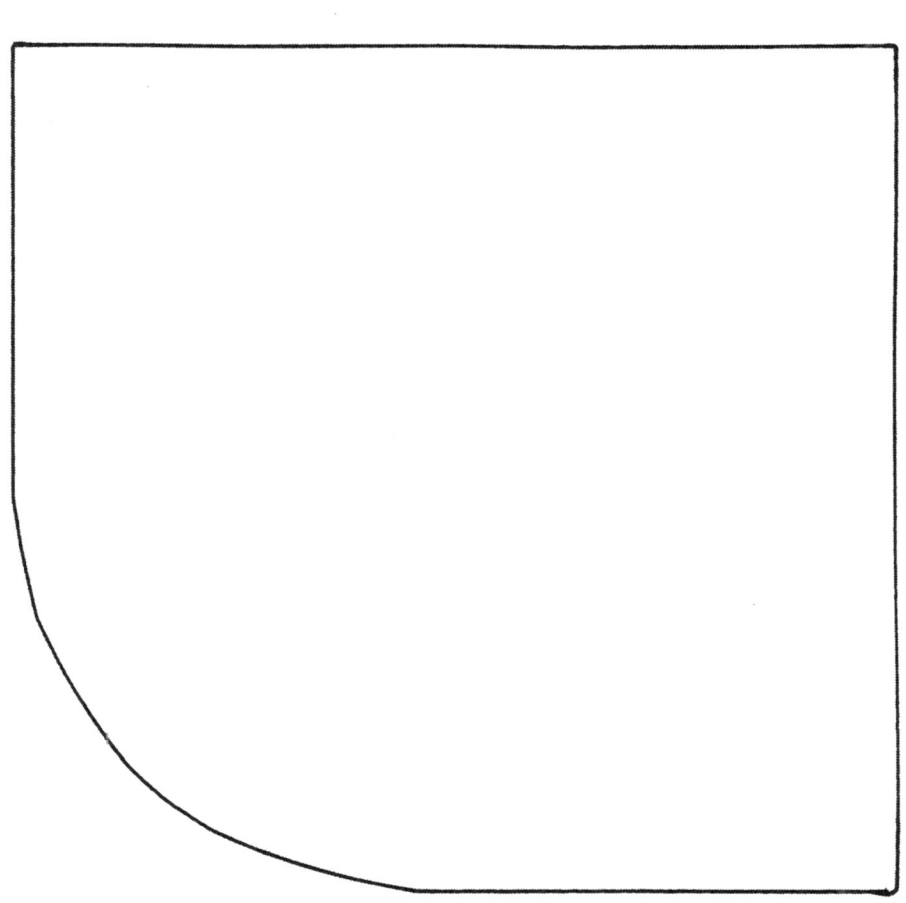

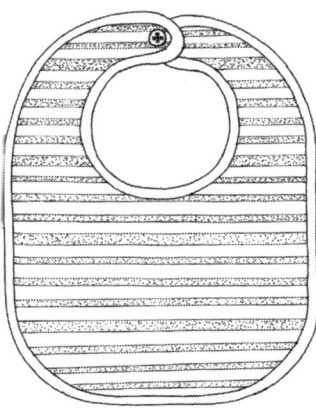

BABY BIB PATTERN

Attach the second pattern piece (page 107) to this piece. See page 78 for project instructions.

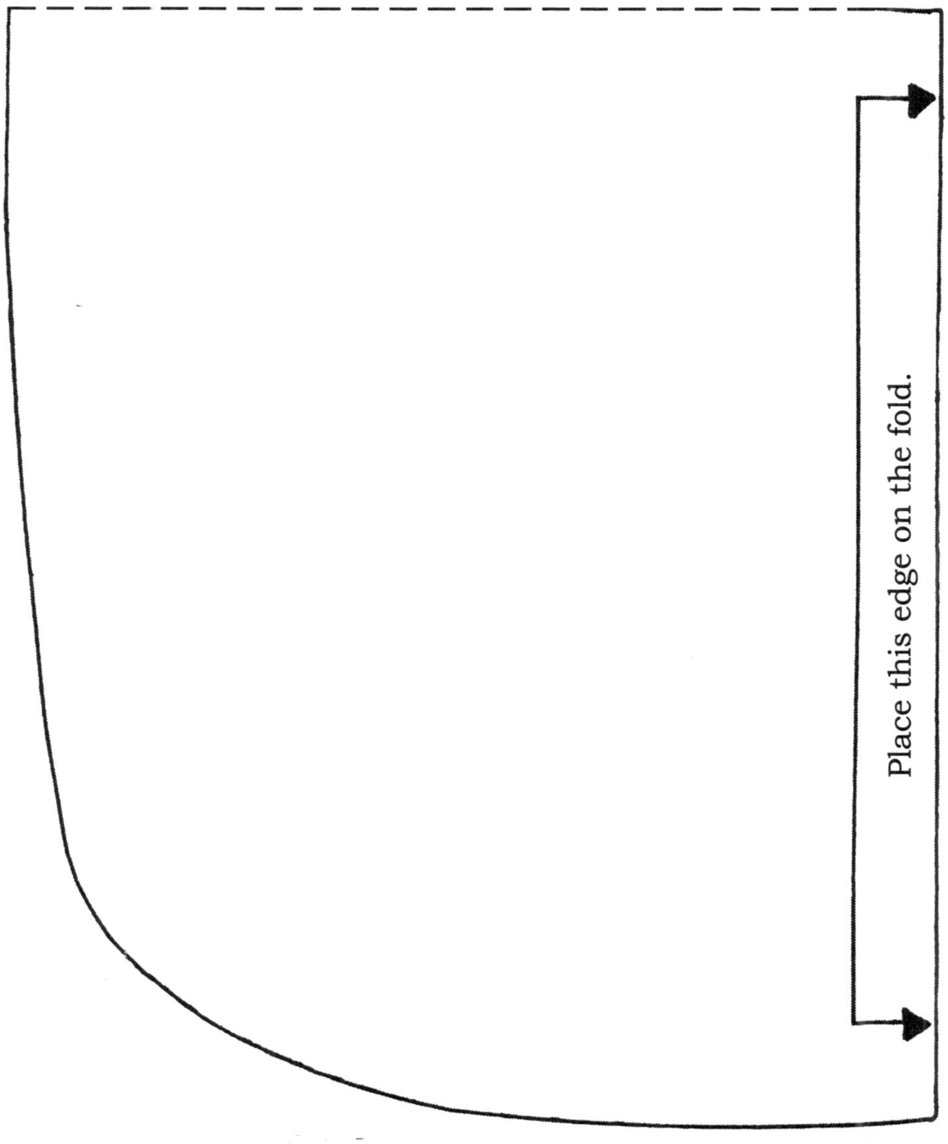

Place this edge on the fold.

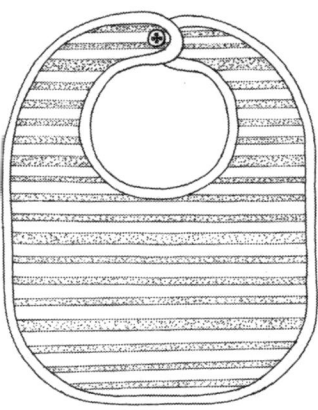

BABY BIB PATTERN

Attach the second pattern piece (page 105) to this piece. See page 78 for project instructions.

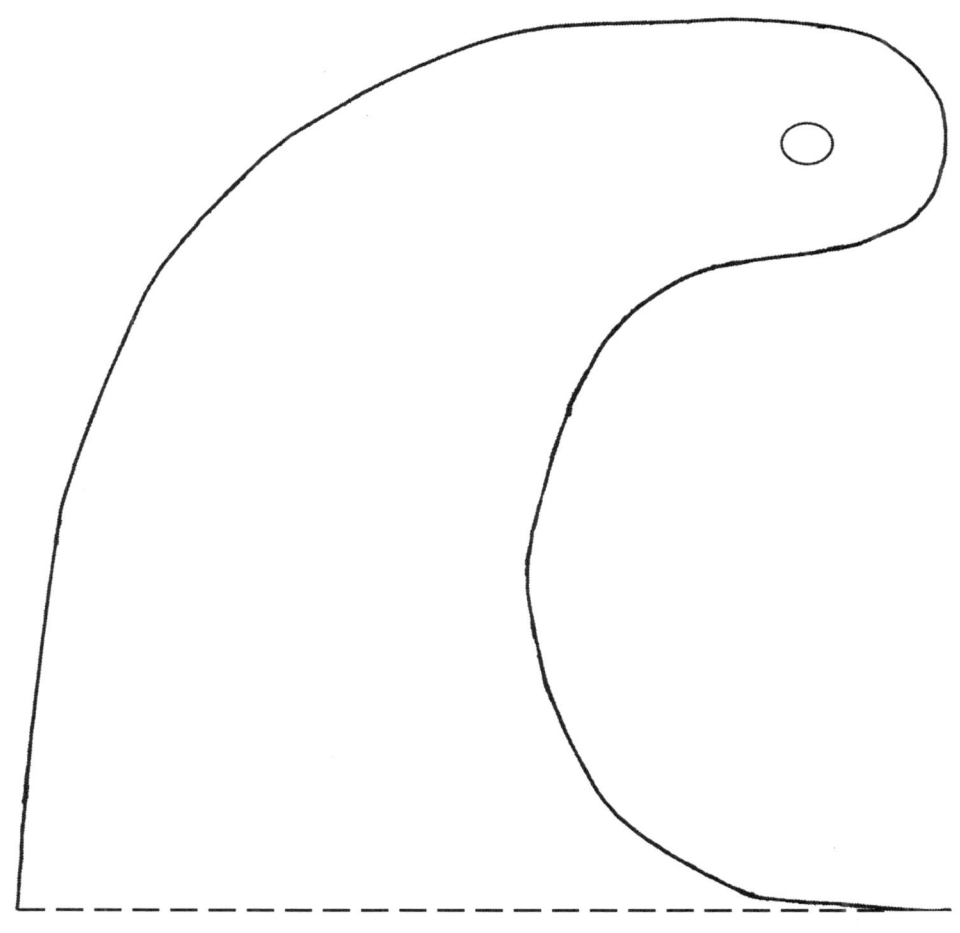

GIFT BAG PATTERN

See page 80 for project instructions.